YOU CAN TURN CONFLICT INTO *Closeness*

7 Communicaton Skills of Successful Marriages

Changes Publishing
1348 Craftsman Ct
Layton Utah 84041

ISBN: 978-0-9861181-0-4

Printed in China

Cover Design by Brooke Elder and Ernest Harker.
Typeset by Michael Cleverly.

Photo credits: Wake boarding photo © Brayden Ball.
Author photo © Wendy Haslam. Used by permission.

For Bulk orders of the book, workbook, ebook, or audio book and any other questions please go to EmilHarker.com

Contents

Acknowledgements

There is no way to measure the influence my wife Teresa has had on everything I have learned. She has been my support every step of the way. Without her, I couldn't have been able to truly understand these principles and practices at the depth required to articulate them.

I mention my three boys, because of the many hours over the past several years it has taken me to write this book. I would like to dedicate this book to them. I hope this book will make their marriages and relationships better because of the time I took to write it.

I acknowledge and appreciate the handfuls of friends and family who have been supportive and encouraging along this long journey. It has not been easy. They have helped me make sure that the ideas and strategies contained in this book are easy to understand to all my readers.

Finally, I acknowledge God. There would be no book without Him. It was His driving force that kept an ADHD therapist focused for over seven years to make this book a reality. If you don't believe in miracles, this is one (just ask my wife).

Real People, Real Results

Jeanette M., Nevada

For thirty years my husband and I had worked and tried very hard to have a successful relationship, but continued to struggle. We had seen several therapists over the years who would help us with communication skills. Our relationship would improve for a time but never lasted. Then we had the good fortune of finding Emil Harker who was different from any therapist we had previously seen. Instead of teaching us communication skills he taught us principles. As we both committed to living these principles our relationship changed. We began to grow stronger and deeper. With Emil's guidance we were able to overcome past hurts and disappointments and were able to achieve an emotional intimacy that we had never before experienced. This was all achieved with a husband who had a hard time expressing his feelings and is not into touchy-feely exercises!

We just celebrated our 38th anniversary and our relationship is still growing stronger as we continue to live the principles Emil taught us. What I learned has not only helped me in my marriage relationship but with all my relationships. I am grateful every single day for what Emil taught me. Emil is a talented and masterful teacher, teaching powerful and effective principles.

Tricia C., Idaho

Our marriage consisted of no communication, lots of silence, fits of anger from me, avoidance and excuses from my husband all resulting in my sleeping away entire afternoons to numb the emotional pain that came from what had become our "happily ever after." I hated what our life had become, broken, hurtful, uncaring and approaching unbearable. I just didn't want a divorce, I wanted to flee as far away as I possibly could from the years of hurt, broken promises, and emotional starvation that was taking place within the supposed sacred confines of our marriage. I went online to search for help. One of the results of my search took me to Emil Harker's website. Without knowing anything about him, I read some of his material and his background and connected with some of the perspective. I could tell that there was something a little different. I knew we needed something special, and I was intrigued. So, I called his secretary and we set up an appointment.

Honestly, I was really hopeful after our first couple of sessions. Emil seemed to know what was going on in our marriage even without us having to tell him very much. He explained how we got to where we were and gave us communication tools and taught us how to use them. One of the tools was "Defining and Accepting Reality." I got really discouraged after our third session. I felt like all that hope was evaporating because nothing was changing. Emil explained that loving my husband was about accepting him the way he was. That idea is nice. However when I heard it I found it repulsive on so many levels. I didn't want to accept him the way he was. I wanted him to be different. I couldn't handle it. I didn't like that he didn't want to spend time with me, or talk with me, or anything. All he wanted to do was play video games. I was dying inside. Emil taught me how by DEFINING AND ACCEPTING REALITY I could be free of the negative energy that was consuming me and create change.

It was really hard but he helped me realize that my attempts to change my husband were not working anyway and that I was going crazy if I kept trying to change him when I couldn't. Something interesting happened when I started truly accepting reality. I can't go into all the details of the process of Accepting Reality because it's hard for me to explain it and much easier for Emil. You will have to read about it in his book to really understand. But when I truly Accepted Reality something interesting happened. Things started to change. Slowly, my husband began learning and applying the principles and started talking differently to me. He showed more effort and intention in connecting with me and really tried to listen to what I was saying, which had become a forgotten attribute in our marriage. I learned principles and communication techniques that empowered me to listen and understand. These principles helped me develop a proper perspective of my husband, myself and why things were the way they were. I began to gain back my ears to hear and the heart to exist in my marriage again.

We are still improving, but now we have an arsenal of tools and education that have strengthened us and helped rise over the bumps in the road when previously we would have been derailed by any little struggle. I guarantee that we would be divorced if we had not been taught the correct principles of communication. Absolutely guarantee it. Without them, my husband would have continued to communicate with me with distance, silence and insincerity, only compounding my anger and resentment towards him. The heavy disappointment that became the foundation of our relationship we had was only going to grow thicker which I could not tolerate much longer. I'm truly grateful that we were somehow lead to Emil. Not only is Emil a powerful educator he is entertaining to talk to and a powerful advocate for healthy communication. Learning these principles not only changed my marriage they changed me.

Terri M., Utah

My sister told me about going to see Emil. It saved their marriage and I needed a serious miracle. I was devastated by what was happening to my marriage and my family. My kids had just moved out of the house not too long ago, and these were the years I was hoping to be able to spend long days with my husband. Unfortunately he had different plans. Desperate, I went to Emil to see if he could save our marriage.

Our marriage was in serious trouble and I felt like it was all my fault because I could see how I hadn't handled things very well. I was working a lot of hours and was grumpy at home. I was being crushed by both guilt and rejection. He helped me see that I could still take responsibility for my stuff and recognize that my stuff was not enough to explain how my husband decided to go a different direction. He helped me develop a healthy perspective so I could cope better. Although my marriage ended, I am a happier healthier person than I ever was. I really like myself and the desperate feelings I had for my ex-husband are much different, and when I put everything in perspective the pain is much less intense. I learned that his desire to search for "greener" pastures wasn't something I was going to change. Emil helped me realize that as much as I love my husband he wasn't the same man anymore. The man he is now isn't the man I wanted to be with anymore. It was very sad in realizing this, but with Emil's help it is more bearable. I'm writing this to explain that these principles work even if it doesn't "save" your marriage. What I found was that if I had "saved" my marriage, all I would have done was postpone both finding myself and my happiness.

Zach C., Utah

I went with my wife to go see Emil because our relationship was falling apart. We had tried therapy in the past, and I was expecting therapy like I've experienced in the past. However, Emil's approach took me completely off guard. After a couple sessions with my wife, Emil turned to my wife and shocked me. He said to my wife right in front of me. "Well, if your husband knows what you want, and you've told him several times, and he thinks that what you are asking is reasonable and yet he still doesn't follow through. What does that mean? What is the reality?" I was dumbfounded and very upset. I felt like I was just thrown under the bus. After that session I walked out and had no intentions of coming back. I talked with my church leader and felt validated. I talked with my dad and got validated. I even went to another therapist and felt validated. I got all of the validation I was looking for, but it didn't change the fact that my wife still wanted out. She moved out of the house and was living with her mom in a different state. Frustrated, desperate, and humbled, I realized that Emil was the only one I knew that knew my wife and knew what it would take to get my wife back.

So, I called him up and asked if he would be willing to see me. He was totally cool. He wasn't offended at all that I was mad at him. He flatly said, that he would do anything he could to help me get my wife back. I realized later that he had already thought through this whole process, how I would probably get mad, and leave but that if I wanted the marriage to work that I would come around. And if I'm honest with myself, I have to admit that all of this had to happen to get my attention. It totally worked.

That session he taught me this principle called "Communicating with the Desired Outcome In Mind" It was so simple. I couldn't figure out how that principle had evaded me all my life. To be honest, I was frustrated that these principles Emil taught me weren't taught to me a long time ago. Anyway, things with my wife happened just as he predicted. I did exactly what he told me to do, and showed me how it fit with applying the principle "Communicating With The Desired Outcome In Mind."

To make a long story short, I liked what I was learning and even more liked what I was becoming. It wasn't about changing just my behavior, I was actually growing and learning how to really connect. I wanted the results to be immediate, and I had to learn more patience. Emil was always coaching me to be patient and trust the principles. I trusted him because everything he was telling me seemed to workout like he predicted. And, now my marriage is better than it ever was. That was a while ago, and now I know that if the relationship is struggling, I just need to remind my self the things Emil taught me and I get back on track. I owe it all to Emil because if it weren't for him, I'd definitely be divorced.

Introduction

> I have been impressed with the urgency of doing. Knowing is not enough; we must apply. Being willing is not enough; we must do.
>
> LEONARDO DA VINCI

There is a difference between knowing how to do something and being good at something. Let me tell you a story that illustrates this point. I was sitting on the couch of this huge house-boat called "Big Dog," docked at Antelope Point Marina in Lake Powell, a beautiful reservoir that spans Southern Utah and Arizona. I was talking with Chandler Higgins, a professional wakeboarder about wakeboarding tricks. He was describing a trick he was working on, and he was using numbers and names I didn't understand. Stopping him before he finished, I said, "I have no idea what you just said." In slight jest, he replied: "I thought you were a wakeboarder, Bro!" I responded "Yeah. I like to wakeboard, but your idea of wakeboarding and mine are way different." I explained that what he was describing was way beyond my experience.

Earlier in the day, as I watched Chandler wakeboard, I realized I was watching an expert. The years of practice had transformed something Chandler could simply do into a remarkable set of skills that evoke awe. One of the tricks he did that looked so awesome was a back flip with a 360° rotation but gainer style off the wake; all while being pulled behind a boat and holding the handle. He called it the "Whirly-bird."

I asked Chandler to write a description of what it is and what it is like for him to do the trick. In Chandler's own words, he describes what only a professional wakeboarder can truly comprehend. Imagine hearing this with a slight "southern California surfer-dude" accent, and you will have channeled into the conversation.

> At the moment the wake is still peaking, the boat still sounding vibrant and alive, I continue up the wake. At the very last second my board is leaving the peaking wake, I heave my chest upwards, bring my shoulders back, take a deep breath and drop my right hand from the handle, and begin to square my body to the wake as well as to the boat. I know the moment I'm airborne that I'm on the perfect path to nailing the "Whirly Bird."
>
> I'm in the air, I'm upside down floating backwards now. I crank my neck to the right to force my head to look over my right shoulder. I need to rotate. To successfully land this trick, I need to add the 360° twist. I remind myself I must keep my composure or my body will be completely and painfully reminded of the technical riding ability required to perform this trick. I pull with my left arm while my body follows through as I keep my eyes looking over my right shoulder. My left arm continues pulling on the handle, whipping me around with the speed of the boat. In just a wink, my body

> comes around facing the same direction it was when I first started the trick on the opposite side of the wake. I grab the handle once again with my right hand and brace myself.
>
> The trick is done, but I haven't landed yet. I am still in the air, beyond the wake, in the flat, smoothness of the deep, cool, blue water. As my legs brace, my mind sets on the same continuing cut through the landing as I had when I took off. I look to where I'm going, not to where I'm landing. I push my chest out, bring my shoulders back, allow the tense muscles to relax in my neck and back, drop the landing gear, and touch the water again with the back end of the board. The water sprays as bent knees absorb the shock of the landing, and the board bites hard into the water. "Nailed it!"
>
> I look back at the wake admiring the magnificent scenery that surrounds me and respecting the fact that not only did I survive, but also I conquered the unseen force in life and in the lake that always reaches up to pull you down, defeat you, destroy you, and take from you that which you hold closest and dearest to your heart.

His poetic description of his successful execution

contrasts sharply with the results I achieved when attempting a complicated wakeboard trick. The easy part was catching big air. The problem was my technical failure in the landing. As a consequence, my left knee buckled, and I severed my ACL.

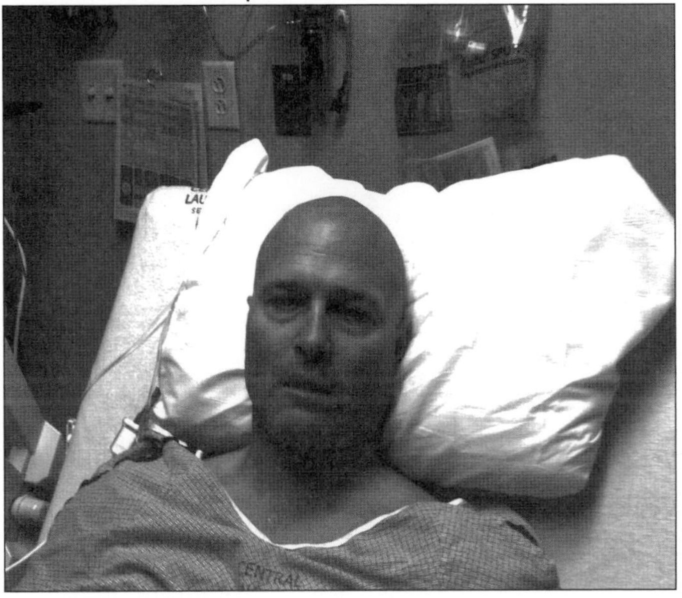

What started out as a fun trip on Lake Powell ended up with reconstructive surgery on my knee at the hospital. Chandler's ability and my unfortunate experience demonstrate the difference in being able to do something and having skill. Being able to talk doesn't actually mean we are good at communicating. We need serious training in communication if we want to successfully navigate the inevitable conflicts in marriage.

Committing to Communicate Effectively

The quality of our relationships is not due to some predetermined sequence in our DNA that programs us to think and respond in certain ways. Instead, being a great communicator is much like being great at wakeboarding or anything else in life. Greatness is the result of learning and applying principles that govern the skill. We have the ability to improve our relationships just like Chandler Higgins nailed the "Whirly Bird"—by learning the principles that govern the skills. Instead of wakeboarder skills, we are talking about communication skills. But just like Chandler, we can avoid damaging crashes by dedicating ourselves to practicing the principles associated with that greatness.

For the past several years, I have been on a quest to find what it takes to help couples experience the love and happiness they believed would grow by uniting in marriage. You know how it is. You are so "in love" that you can't live without each other while you are dating. Then, after the wedding bells and life happens the wheels fall off this "Love Bus." So what happens to that sense of commitment and connection that kept you talking until the wee hours of the morning just to do it all over again the next evening? Unfortunately for most, the dreams of "happily-ever-after" are replaced with "how did we get here?" The fact that over half of all marriages result in disappointment doesn't mean that marital happiness is guarded by fairies and leprechauns.

It is not only possible to create mutually loving and satisfying relationships, I'm going to show you how.

I have developed a refined collection of principles that will help you become a great communicator. I often refer to these principles as commitments because you must commit to practicing and applying the principles presented consistently in order to acquire great communication skills in your marriage. Think about it. Just reading golf magazines and watching golf on television doesn't make you good at golf. And just watching wakeboarding videos on YouTube isn't going to make you great at wakeboarding. Sure, you might get useful information from these sources, but it is the disciplined implementation of the correct principles that govern greatness on a consistent basis that results in skills. The same thing applies to communication. Often I hear that a relationship should be successful because, "I'm a nice guy." Or "I'm a nice person, why isn't our marriage working?" I respond to that question with a question of my own. "What does that have to do with developing successful marriage skills?" Just because you are a nice person doesn't mean you are going to be good at playing the violin. Being a nice person doesn't mean you are going to be able to breakdance or wakeboard. Being nice is not enough. It takes skill.

I don't want to burst your bubble, but mastering the skills is not a guarantee that all of your dreams will come true, no matter what you do. No matter how great of a communicator you are, your partner still has the ability to choose what he or she wants. Unfortunately, there will be some who will choose fear of change over closeness. We can't take that choice away from them. What we can do is eliminate, as much as possible, the barriers we put in the way of our relationship that prevent us from relationship greatness. By following these principles, not only can we change ourselves, we can maximize change in others by learning how to tap into the psychodynamics that magnify our persuasive influence.

This program is not a quid-pro-quo agreement: "I'll do this, if you'll do that." No, it is deeper and more profound. It is "I will do this, no matter what." It is "I give you permission to not be perfect, and I will still love you." This is called unconditional love. Can you imagine not only loving this way but also being loved back this way? That is the vision I want to share with you—the possibility and the realization of this kind of love.

As we take on these commitments and apply these principles on an individual basis, we take on the responsibility that was ours in the first place: to be happy. We prevent ourselves from taking on other people's fears and weaknesses. Through the application of these commitments, we stop defining our value by how others treat us. We see through the negativity of others to their fear, pain, or weaknesses. When we take on these commitments, we become free.

Whether you are still single, newly married and

numb with bliss, married but struggling, or overwhelmed with despair, this program is for you. I invite you to carefully consider these commitments. If you take on these commitments and apply these time-tested principles, I promise you your life will take on greater meaning and more fulfillment and satisfaction than you ever imagined.

Listed below are the 7 Communication Skills of Successful Marriages introduced to you in this book:

1. Assuming Good Intent
2. Defining and Accepting Reality
3. Communicating with the Desired Outcome in Mind
4. Clear, Direct, and Sensitive Communication
5. Killing Criticism
6. Fencing Conflict
7. Disarming Landmines

Throughout the book, you may notice times when some principles are ignored while certain skills are being presented. This is by design because we are dealing with human beings not computer programs or robots. This means that even though we might devote ourselves to the process of improving communication, we are not going to be perfect communicators overnight. Therefore, we need to accept that there will be times when we will be showing our weaknesses more than our strengths. This is a seamless program that doesn't forget the reality of human frailties. In fact, it accounts for these realities. Following the principles and strategies presented in this program, the reader will develop all the skills they need to diminish conflict and increase closeness.

Let's start with the first commitment, a fundamental principle to creating change and the most liberating of them all: ASSUMING GOOD INTENT.

Chapter 1

Assuming Good Intent

> The motivational root of all behavior can be classified into two groups: increased comfort and decreased pain. Increasing pain is not one of them. Most people are doing the best they can. If you assume they aren't, you'll be wrong most of the time.
>
> — Emil Harker

Megan and Tommy are married. Megan has been cleaning the house all day. She has been tidying up the bedroom and putting things away. Tommy comes home from work in a hurry. He changes his clothes, puts on his soccer uniform, and quickly heads to a game. With her arms full of bath towels for the master bathroom, Megan comes into the room and sees Tommy's clothes on the bed, shoes on the floor in the middle of the room, and the bedspread and pillows in disarray. At this point, Megan has a choice. The quality of their relationship for next few days will be determined by how Megan handles this situation. One way will lead to hurt feelings, disappointment, conflict, and distance. The other way will lead to comfort, closeness, and a commitment from Tommy.

Let me begin our discussion of ASSUMING GOOD INTENT by sharing "The Parable of the Neighbor's Apple Tree."

Karl and Bob are neighbors. Karl has an apple tree that sits in the center of his front lawn. It isn't an unusually large apple tree, but in early fall, it is covered with apples—bushels more than Karl can use. Karl usually takes a bushel of apples to Bob and encourages him to help himself to the fruit on the tree. Of course Bob would always wait until Karl had his fill of apples and made sure to show his appreciation for Karl's willingness to share his surplus apples.

For the most part, Bob and Karl get along. They are cordial and wave when they see each other, but both enjoy their privacy as well. Recently Karl made a comment about Bob's dog that starts barking early in the morning.

Karl wasn't really mean about it; he was simply "telling it like it is." In his forthright manner, he told Bob that his dog's barking interfered with his sleep on those rare occasions when he could sleep in and he would appreciate it if Bob would keep his dog quiet a little longer.

> The air was cool and crisp when Bob walked out early one morning to get his newspaper. He enjoyed the quiet solitude of the morning when he could enjoy reading the paper without the distractions of e-mails, phone calls, and texts that pour in signaling the beginning of work time. But what he discovered that morning while fetching the paper came as a surprise. All over his front lawn were apples. He looked at Karl's lawn, and there were no apples. No apples on Karl's lawn where the apple tree grew. No apples…? This didn't make sense.
>
> In the back of Bob's mind there was a flurry of activity as synapse after synapse fired in a successive chain reaction trying to explain what his eyes were seeing. Little did he know that while he was searching through his mind for an explanation there were invisible gremlins in his mind guiding these thought processes. These invisible gremlins could be called beliefs, insecurities, or weaknesses. Guided by invisi-

ble gremlins, explanations that conform to preconceived beliefs, insecurities and weaknesses seem to resonate as the most reasonable options when analyzing any given situation. As a result of this biased thinking process, Bob concluded that Karl was retaliating against him because his dog barks in the morning. No other explanation seemed to make sense. Bob imagined Karl's malicious behavior. In his mind's eye, he pictured his dog barking, and Karl getting out of bed. He pictured Karl just before dawn dressed in pajamas and a robe throwing apples all over Bob's lawn in a childish fit.

Bob's mental movie showed a close up of Karl's vindictive delight as he relished in his retaliation. He saw it so clearly. It made perfect sense. How else could all of the apples be on only Bob's lawn? There was no crazy wind that blew the apples off of the tree and onto Bob's lawn alone. If the wind blew and apples fell, they would be randomly scattered, so there should have been apples on Karl's lawn too.

In fact, there would have been even more apples on Karl's lawn than on Bob's. Fueled by the fear of being taken advantage of and mistreated by his neighbor, Bob dropped his paper, picked up an apple, and

> threw the first of many onto Karl's front lawn.

Hold it. Let's freeze this in 3-D Matrix style. Let's just assume for the moment that Bob is right. Imagine for a second that Bob was able to pull the perfect Sherlock Holmes and deduce Karl's dastardly deed. If Karl was secretly watching out the front window behind the security of the pulled shades while Bob threw apples on his lawn, do you think Karl would come to the front porch and yell out to Bob: "Hey Bob, you figured it out! You got me! I thought I was going to get away with this. But I guess I can't pull the wool over your eyes?" Of course not. Even if Karl stayed up late at night, painted himself with black grease paint like an army commando, and crawled across the lawn tossing all the apples off of his lawn and onto Bob's, he is not going to admit it to Bob. In fact, he will most likely deny he did anything. A more reasonable reaction to Bob throwing apples back on Karl's lawn would be something like, "Hey Bob! What are you doing!?" Even if Bob is right in assuming Karl did this maliciously, it won't change the outcome. He can't prove it's Karl's fault. And if Karl wasn't upset before, he's really going to be upset now.

What if we could rewind the 3-D movie? What if Bob conducted a manual override on his mind-manipulating gremlins and instead of deciding that Karl's behavior was malicious, he insisted there must be a legitimate reason to explain why the apples were on his side of the lawn and not on Karl's side.

Bob begins to explore possible scenarios that could explain how Karl's lawn doesn't have apples and Bob's does. If Bob's explanations are too farfetched, they will have no power to persuade the invisible gremlins of his mind. He can't make up something extraordinary like aliens playing a practical joke because that just wouldn't cut it. Instead he forces himself to come up with a compelling and rational reason. He may not be able to figure out the actual reason, but as long as it is a believable reason, one that could explain why all the apples were on his side of the lawn, he considers it a possible option. The more reasonable the option, the more probable and plausible. As Bob puts energy into exercising his imagination to come up with a reasonable explanation, Bob finds some rationale that there could have been apples all over both lawns, but that Karl had only picked up the ones on his side of the lawn. This could account for why there were only apples on Bob's lawn and not Karl's.

By simply exploring other explanations, Bob finds he isn't as angry with Karl. He is bugged that he has to pick up all the apples from his lawn, but he doesn't blame Karl. Let's reimagine an alternative ending to the parable:

> Wishing the apples weren't there isn't going to make them go away either. Although it's an inconvenience, Bob picks up all of the apples when he gets home from work.

> He cuts and cores the apples and puts them in piecrusts and tosses them into the oven. Forty-five minutes later with the smell of warm cinnamon and spices, Bob takes hot apple pies out of the oven. With apple pie in hand, Bob walks over to Karl's house and knocks on the door. When Karl answers, Bob says: "Hey Karl, this morning I woke up and saw all these apples all over my lawn. I couldn't stand watching them go to waste. I figured you already beat me to picking up your apples from your lawn, and I can't expect you to pick the apples off of my lawn. So with so many apples, I made a couple of pies and thought you might like one."

If Karl truly was innocent, whether Bob's imagined explanation was accurate or not, Karl would see Bob as a good neighbor. There would be a sense of appreciation, not only for Bob's thoughtfulness in the gift of the pie but also because Bob wasn't offended.

But what if Karl was indeed the mastermind of the malicious movement? What if Karl was really trying to upset Bob? Consider how Karl would feel if he stayed up late at night relishing in his apple throwing retaliation and Bob acted like Karl did him a favor. Karl's efforts to get under Bob's skin would have been frustrated. Instead of getting upset Bob had baked him a pie, returning kindness for an insult. By ASSUMING GOOD INtent, Bob foils any attempt Karl may have made to sting Bob. As a result it robbed Karl from any sense of vindication and as a consequence Karl's conscience gives him an internal rebuke for being so childish when Bob was so kind and reasonable.

By assuming good intent, Bob is the master of his mood and an agent of change in others. He is cushioned from the perceived and real weaknesses and insecurities of others and therefore more able to maintain the momentum of a good mood when others are malicious or mindless.

> "When we Assume Good Intent, we understand that rude or hurtful comments or actions are about the sender and actually reflect the character and condition of the person who is being rude or hurtful."

Hurtful behavior of others is the expression of their own hurt, fear, or human weakness. We can avoid the pain of offense when we interpret the behavior of the offender as an expression of their hurt, fear, or weakness. Think about how you might respond to someone who is afraid, hurt, or feels weak. Would you become aggressive if someone presented themselves as weak, hurt, or afraid? Of course not! You would reach out to them, help subside their fears, and comfort them. When we assume good intent, we see through the façade of hurtful behavior. This different perspective acts as an invisible, emotional insulation—a barrier that hurtful behavior cannot penetrate. The potential offender's pain and confusion wasn't ours to take in the first place.

Practicing the principle of assuming good intent helps you develop a psychological cushion without having to get thick skin. It helps you realize your value as an individual is secure. In other words, your self-esteem is secure. Assuming good intent helps you realize that ill treatment from others is about them not you.

It might be helpful to understand how some people develop hurtful communication patterns. Realizing that good-meaning people inadvertently develop less sensitive communication may provide a sense of perspective and help you understand the principle of assuming good intent better.

While growing up, many people learn that sensitivity is synonymous with weakness. If they showed sensitivity to something, their feelings were ignored or, even worse, invalidated. This trained them to disregard their own feelings. As a result they invalidate the feelings of others. For example, a close friend of mine had parents who in their effort to teach strength and resilience downplayed emotions. If their children were sad or upset, his parents told them to "change their attitude" or "snap out of it." His parents said that "Feelings aren't real." His parents didn't know how to deal with emotions or teach appropriate responses. He didn't experience concerned requests from his parents to hear what was wrong or offer to talk to him about the situation. As a result, hurts and fears were stuffed away deep inside. Since emotions weren't validated by his parents, he didn't develop the skills he needed as an adult to express emotions appropriately. He learned to invalidate his own feelings and the feelings of others. Walls were built to protect himself. He didn't develop the skills to honor and express sensitivities, and as a result, he wasn't able to express himself well or respond well when it came to emotions. Unfortunately, he also missed out on a sense of connection that comes from recognizing and responding to sensitivity. He would like to experience this type of closeness, but he is frustrated in his attempts to create it. Worse still, his unskilled efforts to express himself often created more conflict.

Assuming Good Intent

In order to apply the principle of ASSUMING GOOD INTENT, there are three core beliefs you are required to have when considering the intentions of the offender:

1. People want to feel good.

2. People want others to feel good.

3. People are doing the best they can.

As we all have experienced, negativity and rudeness on our part usually brings about a negative or rude response in others. When miffed, bugged, hurt, or surprised by what someone says or does, engage the creative mind in exploring an explanation that stays true to the three core beliefs of ASSUMING GOOD INTENT. Try explaining what the other person did that miffed, bugged, or upset you in a way that makes the other person seem as innocent as a lamb. I encourage you to try this mental exercise and answer these questions. What is the worse thing that can happen? What do you want the outcome to be? More importantly, who do you want to be?

Here is an example that illustrates the use of ASSUMING GOOD INTENT compared to the common communication strategy: Assuming Ill Intent.

Megan and Tommy are married. Megan has been cleaning the house all day. She has been tidying up the bedroom and putting things away. Tommy comes home from work in a hurry. He changes his clothes, puts on his soccer uniform, and quickly heads to a game. With her arms full of bath towels for the master bathroom, Megan comes into the room and sees Tommy's clothes on the bed, shoes on the floor in the middle of the room, and the bedspread and pillows in disarray. At this point, Megan has a choice. She can assume good intent or bad intent on the part of Tommy.

As you consider how you might react if you were Megan, keep in mind the three core beliefs. Which set of beliefs is she going to draw from? Is she going to believe that Tommy doesn't care about her feelings? Will she believe that Tommy doesn't appreciate her efforts to make the home look nice? Will she believe that Tommy is lazy and messy and doesn't want to do his part in helping maintain a clean home? If Megan holds on to these beliefs, she is not ASSUMING GOOD INTENT. (At this point it doesn't matter what the "real" intent is. Even if Tommy is guilty of all the negative assumptions, it doesn't matter at this point. Later we will be discussing what to do if the intention is to hurt, or if Tommy doesn't really care.)

If Megan assumes that Tommy is being lazy or inconsiderate, it will have a huge impact on how she feels and how she approaches him when he gets home from his game—and it won't be pretty. If she is upset, blames, and attacks, Tommy's natural response will most likely be defensiveness. If Tommy is defensive instead of understanding Megan's frustrations, the situation will become worse. As a result, an argument will ensue. Imagine if this interaction seems likely as Tommy gets home from his soccer game.

Tommy: "Hey, Babe."

Megan: "Don't 'Hey, Babe' me! You came home from work and threw your clothes all over the room expecting me to pick them up."

Tommy: "Hey, I didn't ask you to pick them up."

Megan: "Did you think they were magically going to put themselves away? I spend all day cleaning the house and putting things away, and you just add one more thing for me to add on my list of things to do."

Tommy: "I can't believe you are jumping on my case. I was in a hurry and was going to be late. I didn't have time to put everything away and straighten the room before I left."

Chances are that this conversation could easily continue. Tommy feels attacked by Megan, and Megan feels unappreciated and disrespected by Tommy. Both feel completely justified in their different perspectives. The end result of this interaction is going to be more hurt feelings and less closeness, which is more of what they don't want.

But what if Megan applies the principle of ASSUMING GOOD INTENT? If Megan catches herself and replaces her negative belief of Tommy's ill intention with the principle of ASSUMING GOOD INTENT the outcome will be completely different.

Let's imagine a scenario where Tommy gets home from the soccer game and walks in and greets Megan who is reading on the couch. Let's imagine how the interaction between Tommy and Megan might be different if Megan applies the principle, ASSUMING GOOD INTENT.

Tommy: "Hey, Babe."

Megan: "Hey, how was your game?"

Tommy: "It went really well, I only got scored on twice. That's an improvement from last game, and the guys tell me that the team we played tonight was better than the last one."

Megan: "Good for you babe." *(Apologetically)* "Hey, I started getting upset when I saw your clothes on the bed and the bed all messy after you left to your game, but then I realized that you were in a real hurry so you didn't have time to put your clothes away before you left, so I put your stuff away for you. Did you make it to your game on time?"

Tommy: "Yeah, uh sorry about that. Yeah I was in a hurry, but I made it just in time. And thanks for taking care of all my stuff. I was planning on doing it when I got home. I owe you big time."

When Megan Assumes Good Intent, Megan still gets to tell him she was upset that he left his clothes all over the place and the bed in disarray, but she does it in a way that makes it hard for him to get defensive.

There are some who may say to themselves: "Hey! That's not fair! Tommy shouldn't have left his clothes on the bed." That's absolutely predictable. I don't blame you one bit. I want you to keep that thought in your mind. The next few chapters will deal with this idea. When we Assume Good Intent, we are not saying that it's OK for Tommy to leave his clothes on the bed and expect Megan to pick up after him.

The point in ASSUMING GOOD INTENT is to minimize getting hurt and maximize power and influence when something happens. In this scenario, Megan accomplishes this when she assumes good intent. Can you see how ASSUMING GOOD INTENT actually made the interaction better? Take into consideration the alternative to not ASSUMING GOOD INTENT. Do you really think that if Tommy really loves Megan, he will take advantage of her or mistreat her? If Tommy doesn't really care about Megan's feelings, then Megan will be having a very serious talk with Tommy, but that is the exception and will be dealt with in a different chapter. In this case, we are working with Tommy who truly wants the best for Megan. The last thing he wants is to make Megan mad because, let's face it, if Megan gets upset, Tommy's life is going to be more difficult. Another point that is often overlooked is the fact that the person who suffers the most is the person who is assuming ill intent. Think about it. While Tommy is having a great time playing soccer, Megan is stewing at home and is miserable. ASSUMING GOOD INTENT is not only good for the individual, Megan in this case, but it is great for the couple.

> "It is helpful to assume good intent all the time, even when the other person is being malicious on purpose."

Because people don't want to be duped or taken advantage of, people ask how they should handle situations when someone is really trying to be rude, manipulate, or take advantage of them. What do you do when someone is *trying* to be malicious? Assume Good Intent anyway. Remember the reasons people are mean, rude, or hurtful is because they are responding to fear, hurt, or human weakness. Assuming good intent is being kind and loving and allows you to operate on a positive framework rather than a negative one. By applying assuming good intent, you will be more positive, more powerful, and more persuasive. You will have better health. You will be more pleasant to be around. Think about it. Who do you like to be around? Do you like to be around people who are positive and give room for potential growth or around people who always think that everyone has some angle and everything is suspicious?

Assume Good Intent All the Time

Sometimes we can't always tell when someone is being cruel. What may sound mean may really be an attempt to be helpful or to get help. Our assumptions and beliefs determine our emotions. Emotions motivate behavior. What we do to make relational interactions more positive is the result of challenging our beliefs about people—specifically our beliefs about our spouse.

Assuming good intent isn't normal. Explaining the motivation of the behavior of the other person when they have said or done something that came across hurtful or offensive as if the other person was trying to do something noble, or good, or avoid anything bad in any way sounds crazy because it seems completely unnatural. However, if you take a closer look, wouldn't it be safer to say that you and your spouse really do want what is best for each other? Don't you think you and your spouse try to avoid saying things that will hurt each other? You don't bring up issues just to bring up something to fight about. You love each other. You want what is best for each other. And since that is the case, wouldn't it make sense to maintain that belief all the time? Even when it *seems* like the other person is being mean? If we believe that our spouse truly wants what is best for us, we will be right when we Assume Good Intent much more often than not. If you assume good intentions and you are right, you win. If you assume good intentions and you are wrong, you still win. You win because you reduce being offended when offense wasn't intended. The person who is less offended and less stressed is more empowered. The outcome leads to less stress in life, less hurt, less arguments, and greater closeness. Can you imagine two people committing to this one principle alone? What a difference it would make!

To reiterate, *assuming good intentions* in others doesn't make the other person's behavior right or acceptable. You don't *assume good intentions* to protect or justify the person who is being insensitive or malicious. ASSUMING GOOD INTENT gives you a platform to discuss issues in a positive and optimistic format. ASSUMING GOOD INTENT is like non-stick coating of the heart that doesn't let the other person's hurtful behavior stick. Hurtful behavior is about the person being hurtful. If you or someone you know is in an abusive relationship, they may need to get outside help to break the cycle. It is important to note that the person doing the abusing is just as stuck as the person being abused.

When your spouse says or does something that hurts, bugs, miffs, or upsets you, explain their behavior supporting the belief that they:

1. Want to feel good (or avoid pain)

2. Want you to feel good (or avoid pain)

3. Are doing the best they can

Remember: Any explanation that comes across as selfish, thoughtless, or inconsiderate will not count.

To make the skill a little easier to develop, a helpful hint is to imagine what your spouse might say if you asked if their intention was to hurt you or make your life more difficult. Most likely they will give you an explanation, a reason, or justification for what they did—and hurting was not their objective. If it was their objective to hurt you, they are really trying to get your attention or help you understand something. Think of times when you hurt someone you cared about by something you did or didn't do. Of course you had good intentions. Also, think of times when you did something on purpose to hurt your spouse. What were you really trying to communicate? What did you really want to have happen? I'm confident you didn't want to have more problems and less closeness. Most likely you were trying to make a point, help them see how hurt your were, or protect yourself. So, if you get stuck trying to see through someone's seemingly hurtful behavior to find their good intentions, try looking at times when you have been hurtful. You just might find the magic clue to see into their soul.

Here is another example of a person applying the principles of ASSUMING GOOD INTENT. She writes this process out in order to stick with the process. In this scenario the wife is bugged that her husband comes home from work late a lot. She writes:

"My husband comes home from work late almost every day and doesn't call me to let me know he is going to be late."

She then explains his behavior such that: 1) He wants to feel good, 2) He wants her to feel good, 3) He is doing the best he can. This may take some creativity, and at first it may sound farfetched. But, she sticks with the rules. She explains why her husband doesn't come home from work on time and includes why he doesn't call.

> "My husband really wants to come home on time and really tries to. He is also really devoted to his job and wants to feel secure in his employment, so he tries to get those last few things done before he comes home. He is always running late trying to get one more thing done. He wants to make sure he provides for us for the long term, so he stays late to show his commitment to his job and make sure his employers appreciate him. He doesn't take the time to call me because he can't talk on the phone and get things done at the same time and he is already hurrying as fast as he can, so it would delay him even more. Another reason he may not take the time to call is because he doesn't want to create conflict between us. He knows I am likely to just get upset when he calls to tell me he is running late. He feels bad that he isn't able to come home when he would like, and he hates it when I give him so much pressure about it."

Notice how this process of explaining *why he is late and doesn't call*, doesn't change his behavior. It doesn't say it's OK it just reduces the emotional reaction that comes from taking offense. At the end of this process, she is probably closer to the truth. She realizes that the issue of him coming home late isn't about him not caring about her. It isn't that his work is more important to him than she is. It isn't that he is being lazy or inconsiderate. He really does care about her. She realizes that the reason he comes home late and doesn't call is that he wants to take care of the family, and he is struggling to manage his boundaries. In this case ASSUMING GOOD INTENT may be all that is required to resolve this issue. It could reduce the pain the wife experiences when compared to how she feels when she assumes ill intent. However, if she really wants him to make a stronger effort to coming home earlier, ASSUMING GOOD INTENT will help her confront this issue without being too focused on her emotions of feeling unimportant[1].

ASSUMING GOOD INTENT may seem difficult at first. But it can develop into first nature with a little bit of effort and planning and practice. You will notice the more you practice this principle that ASSUMING GOOD INTENT becomes a part of who you are and what you do.

To reiterate, ASSUMING GOOD INTENT doesn't excuse irresponsible or disrespectful behavior. It does not make

[1]There are going to be many times when behaviors really need to change. ASSUMING GOOD INTENT is a building block to another component COMMUNICATING WITH THE DESIRED OUTCOME IN MIND which will be covered in chapter 3, which will teach you how to maximize change.

what others do good or right. It acts like a magical set of eyeglasses to help you see deeper into the situation, which can help prevent you from taking things personally. Assuming good intent provides you a platform to approach issues in a powerful, positive, and optimistic manner. When you combine assuming good intent with the next principle, defining and accepting reality you will uncover hidden avenues of opportunities to maximize change.

Chapter 2

Defining and Accepting Reality

> When I argue with reality I lose–but only 100% of the time.
>
> BYRON KATIE

As Jared shuts the door and walks to his truck in the driveway, Sandy crumples to the floor behind the closed door, trying to stifle the tears. Jared just shakes his head in frustration as he gets in his truck and heads out to the club to spend time with his friends.

It's the same argument each week. Sandy wants Jared to spend time with her on the weekend and Jared needs the night with friends at the club to wind down from the week. Although this has been going on for years, the weeks are getting rougher for the couple. They struggle more getting along during the week. Jared looks forward more to the weekends when he can take off and relax, and Sandy dreads the weekends where she can't help but feel rejected. Between muffled sobs, she acknowledges to herself the fact that she can't keep going on like this. Things are getting worse. "If things don't change soon…" She doesn't allow herself to finish the thought.

Many couples wish things could be different in their marriages. This idea is not necessarily a problem. In fact, the desire to make things different is the force that drives change. Believing that things should be different than they actually are becomes problematic, however, when people don't adjust their path to accommodate reality. In other words, if people make decisions based on how they believe things *should* be rather than how they *actually* are, they are acting on information that isn't real. Byron Katie in her book *Loving What Is* describes a fantastic process of helping people reclaim their power by defining and accepting reality.

Defining and accepting reality is a two-step process that unlocks your mind to find peace in what you can't change and find solutions to problems in your life you can.

Step 1: Identify Reality. What is happening or what has happened that bothers you? What is the likelihood that this behavior will continue?

STEP 2: Plan for what you can predict.

Consider the parable of "The Man and the Hole in the Sidewalk."

> Imagine a guy walking down the sidewalk. Further ahead in the direction he is walking he sees what looks like a huge hole in the middle of the sidewalk. Next to what looks like a huge hole is a pile of dirt the size of a car. As he gets closer, he notices that there isn't any police tape or orange traffic cones or barrier to warn people of the danger. He says to himself: "This is ridiculous. They should cover the hole up with boards or set some barricades or something around that hole so people who are walking on the sidewalk don't fall in." Instead of changing directions he continues to walk toward the hole telling himself how someone *should* have done something.

If the man in this story continued walking and ended up falling in the hole, wouldn't we question his level of intelligence? I mean what kind of person sees a potential problem and then continues forward without changing their direction? The answer is surprising. Everyone.

In psychology there is a special term used to describe a person who believes in things that aren't real. We say that person is delusional. No offense, but the truth is that we are all delusional from time to time. For example, consider the parents who believe that their four year old son or fifteen year old son for that matter should go to bed the first time he is asked. Or the parents who believe that their teenage daughter should be responsible and finish her homework before she asks to hang out with her friends. How about people who believe their spouse should know what they want without them having to tell them?

In each of the situations, there are supportive beliefs that keep the delusion alive. For example, the belief that the four year old or fifteen year old should go to bed without fighting is supported by the belief that going to bed is something that happens every night around the same time, so the kids *should* know this and anticipate it. The belief that the teenage daughter should get her homework done before asking to hang out with friends is supported by another belief that since she knows that this is the rule, she *should* remember and follow it.

> “No matter how committed people are to their beliefs, even if the beliefs seem completely reasonable, believing something doesn't actually make it real.”

So if we are all delusional, what is the problem? The

problem with all delusions is that they lead to disappointment and frustration. And when frustration and disappointment are expressed (usually in the form of sarcasm or criticism), the receiver perceives this as an attack and reacts. Just like a nuclear bomb, where a chain reaction occurs creating a chemical explosion when two people are caught up in a chain reaction of hurt and frustration, destructive conflict can blow up and damage a relationship. The principle of DEFINING AND ACCEPTING REALITY is designed to protect you and empower you.

Ironically, accepting reality is a vital step in making things different. Make no mistake, accepting reality does not imply that we smile ignorantly and agree or support what is going on. For example, child sexual abuse is a reality. Accepting this reality does not imply, in any way, that child sexual abuse is OK. Accepting the reality of child sexual abuse is admitting that it is happening, and the consequences are terribly damaging to anyone involved. That is the reality. Once you have defined reality, you then can decide what you are going to do about it. Defining reality is seeing things as they are. Accepting reality is planning for it, and doing something about it. If you don't accept reality, you can't do anything to make a difference.

In the case of child sexual abuse, you might want to warn your neighbors with a list of registered sexual offenders in your area. Perhaps you might decide to not allow your children to have sleepovers. Perhaps you will be more vigilant in knowing where your children are at all times. This is accepting reality. By accepting reality and doing something about it, you actually create a new reality. The new reality is a result of what you do when you accept what is real. Sexual abuse still happens, but based on your choices, the likelihood of it happening to your child and other children is reduced by your decisions. This is how accepting reality doesn't make something morally OK. It also shows how accepting reality is the platform and prerequisite for creating change. If you do not accept reality you have no power. Wishing things were different, or complaining about how things are is an ineffective strategy to create change. Paradoxically, if you want to create change, accept reality.

Before accepting reality is *defining* reality. Reality is a snap shot or assessment of what is happening or what is going on in a situation—not what you want things to be or how you *feel* things are. Defining reality is an assessment of the facts of the situation. When defining reality, we describe the situation or events as they are. This is very objective and scientific. In a relationship defining reality is defining the behavior and the sequence of the behavior. Be careful not to interpret the meaning of the behavior; we are just defining the behavior. For example if you are the wife and you think that your spouse is mad, instead of assuming he is mad describe the actual behavior. "He is very quiet tonight. When he looks at me, his brow is furrowed. When I ask questions, his answers are very short." By pointing out what you see and hear you are separating the subjective interpretation from the objective reality. You just might find out that instead of being mad, the he may just have a bad headache. Insisting that your husband is mad when he actually has a headache could be a catalyst for an argument. A strategy for dealing with this situation is to describe the behavior and then check in. For example: “Hey babe I noticed that you’ve been really quiet tonight, and your brow is all pinched up and furrowed. Are you alright?” Getting good information is a way to clear up misunderstanding and create a connection.

To illustrate DEFINING AND ACCEPTING REALITY consider this interesting example. I was looking through an architecture magazine one day. On the cover of the magazine, I saw a beautiful photo of a mountainside that highlighted a flat, rock lookout point. On the adjacent page, the same photo angle was taken, but the photo was taken after a house was built in that exact spot. The house was built on the side of the mountain such that the rock was inside the house. The architect did not move the rock. The house was designed around the rock. The rock was the rock. It was not a table. It was not a couch. It was the rock. Sometimes we have a rock in our lives, and we would like it to be a chair or a table or a couch. Instead it is a rock.

Sometimes there are sharp edges on the rock and the walls are too close to go around the rock without risking getting hurt. In these situations, there are only four options. The first option is to complain and wish things were different. This is expressed by asking the rock to be a chair or table or lamp or whatever it is you wish it to be and see where that ends up. The second option is to see if you can restructure the house by moving some things around—doing some remodeling to make better accommodations for the rock. If every attempt to make accommodations proves unsuccessful, and life seems to get more uncomfortable, or it isn't enough to make life better, you have two other options. You can do what it takes to get the rock out of the house, or you can move. Can you think of any other options?

This is a simplification of something that is usually so overly complicated by emotions and the situation that it is difficult to see how simple the options are. I say *simple*, not easy: anyone who has ever been in a situation like this knows there is nothing easy about it.

People often get confused when their spouse says one thing and does something else. They don't know what to believe. It is necessary for some people to recognize the difference between what a person *says* is important to them and what really *is* important to them. We can identify what people want and what is important to them by looking at their patterns of behaviors. We can know what people want, but we may not know why.

For example, consider the scenario with Sandy and Jared. If Jared has a pattern of going to nightclubs on the weekends with his friends in spite of his wife telling him that she would like him to spend more time with her, it can be easily deduced that he would rather spend time with his friends on the weekends at the nightclubs than spend time with her. That is defining reality. What we don't know is why? There may be a reason for this, but that doesn't change the fact that when the weekend comes, he is most likely going to be hanging out with his friends instead of spending time with Sandy. This is true even if he were to *say* that she is more important to him than his friends. The reality is that he prefers to spend his time with friends at the nightclub than be with her on the weekends. The common mistake is for the wife to believe that since she believes that her husband *should* want to spend time with her that he will. Believing he *should* spend time with her instead of choosing to spend the weekends with his friends at the nightclub could be absolutely true when we think of using the term *should* as a moral or value position.

The problem comes when she takes *should* to mean "that which she can expect to happen." So, when Friday afternoon rolls around, and she is expecting him to stay home with her instead of going with his friends, she is most likely going to be disappointed.

Metaphorically speaking, she just stepped into the hole. She can predict that he will go with his friends, yet she is planning on him to stay home with her. That is delusional.

Just because she believes that he *should* want to spend time with her on the weekends instead of hanging out with his friends, doesn't actually change the fact that he would rather be with his friends. There is far more evidence to support the belief that he will most likely be with his friends than with her. She has defined the reality, but she hasn't accepted it yet.

The word *should* is what makes things very confusing. The word *should* is a word that represents a person's position of value on a subject or situation. And that's where people get stuck. Just because something morally *should* be different doesn't mean it *will* be different.

I'd like to invite you to expand the meaning of the word *should* a little bit to avoid falling into the pit. When we can accept that the word *should* is a moral or value position that represents something that may or may not happen, rather than of something that does happen, we can be more prepared to accept things as they are and change our course of action when what we want to happen doesn't happen. We went over this in the "hole in the sidewalk" scenario.

> "For the sake of your own sanity, include in your definition of *should* the meaning 'that which probably won't happen.'"

Although there are many things that should happen that do happen, the *should's* that are brought up in relationship interactions are usually brought up in the context of things that aren't happening. People don't talk about things that *should* happen when they *do* happen.

They talk about things that *should* happen when they *don't* happen.

With this additional definition, the wife in the previous story can say to herself: "I can predict that my husband will want to hang out with his friends instead of me this weekend because four out of five weekends he chooses to spend time with his friends even when we have made plans to spend the weekend together. Therefore, it is safe for me to anticipate him bailing out on me to hang out with his friends." This is the transition from defining to accepting reality. Once she accepts reality, she can start exploring options on how she is going to deal with this. When she starts planning on what she can predict, that is when she is accepting reality

It is surprising how powerful and influential people can be when they start accepting reality. The important factor is the act of accepting reality is a game changer. No longer is she stuck expecting something that isn't going to happen. There are three options in the Jared and Sandy scenario. I am going to simplify, but that doesn't actually make it easy. Sandy's first option is to continue to complain and keep hoping her complaints will cause a change in Jared. Second, she can embrace and accept reality. In this scenario, she can plan for and expect that he is most likely going to the night club on the weekends. This does not mean that she surrenders her will and tries to convince herself that she doesn't care. She will seek to understand him better and explore solutions in a kind and loving manner. She may explore what she is or isn't doing that makes him want to spend more time with his friends and then talk about it with him. In the meantime, she will find a way to create an enjoyable weekend that she can look forward to. She will focus on what is working in the relationship not on what isn't. She will work on creating connections with him so she will not be so negatively affected when he goes to the nightclub. Third, as a last resort, if she has tried the first two, and she truly can't seem to find a way to be happy, she owes it to herself to lovingly get out of the relationship. On very rare occasions, this is an option. But it is the last resort option.

Here is another example of DEFINING AND ACCEPTING REALITY:

A client of mine (let's call him Ted) was really stressed out. In fact, he worked himself into a frenzy. He and his wife, Sara, had separated, and it was causing him a lot of grief. He realized that he was making a lot of poor decisions, including taking his wife for granted. When his wife asked for a separation, it was the slap to the head he needed to get on track. After seeing him individually for several weeks, he began to make some progress. He devoted himself to becoming the husband that he should have been all along. And he was doing great!

During conjoint therapy sessions with his wife, Sara would say that she really wanted the relationship to work. At first these statements were encouraging. It provided a source of hope for Ted during a very stressful time. However, over time the statements Sara was making weren't being backed up with behavior. She was warm and then cold then warm again. He explained that he felt like he was losing his mind. He was trying to reconcile what his wife was saying with what she was doing. It was during this time, he said he believed that his wife was just punishing him for all the stupid things he did while they were together. He was going crazy. Sara would be nice and would call him and even let Ted take her out on dates. She was still saying she was hoping their relationship would get better. He was confused because he didn't understand why she hadn't invited him back home. He was frustrated with what was going on. Unfortunately, every time he brought it up, Sara would just say that she was hoping they could be a happy couple again.

I asked him if he would describe the situation as if a researcher were watching them interact together. What would the researcher see and then what deductions would he make. (This is the defining reality part.) He struggled at first. "If I were a researcher, I would think that this guy is a real idiot. First, I am doing all the work and making real changes. Sara isn't doing anything really. Sara makes comments on the changes I've made, but she isn't working on getting back together. She just gives me permission to take her on a date as if she is doing me a favor." After a long pause, he continued, "Her words are saying she wants to be a couple again, but her actions say she just wants to be friends. She is nice, but she's nice like I'm a brother visiting from out of town, not nice like husband and wife nice. The reality is that she wants to get along and for us to be nice to each other, but she really doesn't want a husband/wife relationship."

Defining reality from an objective perspective exposed reality. He didn't want to accept it, but the proof was irrefutable. The more he tried to ignore that she had moved on, the more uncomfortable and strained the relationship became. At this point he began to accept reality. In spite of what Sara said, her actions were saying something completely different. I explained that it is wise to understand what people say, but only believe what people do. As he grasped the reality of his situation, I decided to add the principle of ASSUMING GOOD INTENT to guide him to a position where he could see things more clearly. I asked him if he could explain, using the ASSUMING GOOD INTENT principle, why his wife seemed to be so inconsistent—cold, warm, then cold again. At first he just said it was confusing and that she was just messing with his mind. I encouraged him to pretend for a minute that she really wasn't being mean and that she had good intentions.

With a little bit of help, he realized that she too was confused, and she too couldn't figure it out. Then he paused and thought out loud. "Well as much as I don't want this to be true… maybe she isn't sure she wants things to work out. Maybe she has moved on, but she thinks that she should try to make things work out between us for the kids, but maybe for her own happiness, she doesn't. I mean, that could explain how sometimes she is being nice and how at other times she seems so cold." He realized that she wasn't really messing with his mind after all. In fact, she was just trying to figure things out herself and was just as confused as he was.

A couple weeks later Sara proved this to be true when she said that there was a part of her that wanted everything to be good between them, but the other part of her had already moved on. (She was actually dating someone else while they were going to counseling.) Accepting reality was an important step in helping Ted begin to heal and move on, even before Sara was able to verbalize what was going on in her own life. As painful as this was to hear, the blow was softened because he had already figured it out.

In this example, we used ASSUMING GOOD INTENT to help DEFINE REALITY. Combining the two commitments helps us more accurately see what is going on and understand the situation more clearly. With a clearer perspective of things as they are, we are more able to make decisions with confidence. With a greater awareness of reality and the commitment of accepting it, we are empowered and can change the way we experience the situation.

How to apply "Defining and Accepting Reality"

Ask yourself the following questions:

1. Are you surprised by your spouse's behavior in this situation?
2. Do you have any evidence that would suggest that your spouse's behavior would be different in this situation?
3. Is there anything that you can do about what happened or about the choices that your spouse already made?
4. If the behavior of your spouse is new and uncharacteristic, what might explain this uncharacteristic behavior?
5. If the behavior is characteristic, what would make you think your spouse would act differently?
6. Why does your spouse continue that behavior?
7. What does it tell you about your spouse if that behavior continues?

It is not enough to just ask the questions. You need to answer them. If your spouse's behavior is consistent, you can safely assume that that behavior will continue. The more consistent the behavior is, the more confident you can be that the behavior will continue. If your spouse responds a certain way 90% of the time in a given situation, it would be reasonable to predict that the behavior in that situation is likely to happen 90% of the time. After you have analyzed the situation, you can explore options to prepare for the next time you are in that same situation. Identifying reality is giving yourself permission to see things as they really are, not how you believe they should be. After you have defined the reality, then you can move on to accepting it.

In situations where you are miffed, bugged, hurt, or offended, describe, without emotion, what happened as if you were narrating to someone who is blind. What happened? Be careful not to read into things. Describe it as if you were a spy watching through binoculars and listening through a wiretap. What words were used? What was the tone? What was the body doing? Describe the movements of the hands, eyes, hips, and the facial expression. It might be helpful to try taking the perspective that you were the other person's attorney. In other words use statements that aren't accusatory. If you were the other person's attorney you wouldn't exaggerate anything that would make your client look bad. There would be no hint of sarcasm. Instead the tone of the conversation would be done to protect the goodness of the client.

Compare these two statements and see which one seems less accusatory. "I tried talking to my husband while he was working on his computer, and he totally tuned me out. It must be really hard for him to hear things he doesn't want to hear when he is working on his computer." Compare that with this. "I tried talking to my husband while he was working on his computer. He didn't even acknowledge that I said anything. Even though I was close enough for him to hear me, it didn't register that I was speaking with him. This is something that happens quite a bit. When he gets engrossed in something, he tunes everything out so he can focus on what he is working on."

Notice, how when the wife focuses on the reality instead of the emotion, the emotion changes. The reality doesn't change; her interpretation changes. If she knows it is a common occurrence for him to tune out all distractions from something he is working on, it would be pretty ridiculous for her to expect him to hear her when she knows he's tuned everything out. If she ignores what she knows she figuratively keeps walking even though she knows there is a hole in the side walk. Accepting reality is doing something about it. She could touch him to get his attention and wait for him to make eye contact. She could raise her voice. She could keep saying his name over and over again until he finally looks up from his computer in aggravation. Of course, some options produce better results than others, but her options are only limited by her imagination. No matter how much she tries to convince herself that he *should* be able to hear her when she talks and have it register in his mind, obsessing on *shoulds* will only lead to frustration and disappointment.

Defining and accepting reality is managing expectations based on reality. When you can define reality, you can predict behavior.

> "When you can predict, you can prepare."

If you can predict, but you choose not to prepare and instead complain about the way things are, then you are delusional and will fall into the hole. By defining and accepting reality, you can make personal changes that can actually change the situation. Assuming good intent and defining and accepting reality are building blocks to communicating with the desired outcome in mind. In the next chapter, you will be taught how to construct a statement or request in such a way as to get the other person to drop their defenses and really listen to what you are saying and then do something about it.

Chapter 3

Communicating with the Desired Outcome in Mind

> Begin with the end in mind.
>
> Stephen R. Covey

Jen sits down at the kitchen table with a stack of bills in front of her, and she looks over at Mike who is half asleep with the TV still on. When I say that Jen is looking at Mike, I use the term *look* very loosely. If Jen's eyes could shoot laser-beams at Mike, then Mike would have two holes burned in the back of his head.

Jen: "Mike, are you going to come over

here and work on this with me, or what?"

Mike: *(Groggy)* "Honey, I'm sorry but I am exhausted. I've had a really long day. Can we do it some other time?"

Jen: "Fifteen minutes ago you were wide awake until I told you that we needed to spend a little time on our budget and our finances. Now you're too tired. Seriously, Mike. I'm tired of this. This happens every month. Every time I mention the word budget or finances, you seem to get exhausted."

Mike: "I'm sorry. I hit a wall. I don't understand why you want my help anyway. You definitely don't need it."

Jen: "What's that supposed to mean?"

Mike: "Nothing. Look, I'm tired. I don't want to fight with you. I'm just going to go to bed. I promise I will go over this with you later if you want me to."

Jen: *(As Mike walks to the bedroom)* "The bills aren't going to wait Mike."

When Jen asked Mike to come to the table to help her with the monthly budget and finances, I don't think she wanted this outcome. There is a belief that all we have to do is communicate what we want. That's great when you are ordering from Burger King, but it's not that effective when you are talking with your spouse. When you want something to happen, what you do and what you say can make all the difference.

Imagine how ridiculous your house would look if you decided one day to build it yourself—without the benefit of a blueprint. You went to the local hardware store, bought some wood, and just started nailing boards together. It sounds like a scene out of the Three Stooges. The chaos alone would be comical. This is the very reason building permits are required. If you tried this, you would end up with a big mess.

If you want to build the house of your dreams, it's going to take some forethought and planning. First, you might consider what you want your house to look like. You also might want to consider what you want in your house: How many bedrooms? How many bathrooms? Do you want a walk-in closet in the master bedroom? How about a "his and her" shower? You might think about what you want in the kitchen, the game room, or the living room. What views do you want to have from your living room? Face the mountains, or the lake? After all of this and so much more, you would take these ideas to an architect to draw up a blueprint for a contractor to turn your dream house into a reality. Paint colors, furniture, and even cupboards and door handles can be picked out before the hole is dug and the concrete foundation is poured, but only if there is first a blueprint.

The point is, no matter how great the wood is or how expensive or luxurious the fixtures are, without a solid plan for putting the materials together, the outcome will be disastrous. Communication preparation and building a house has a lot in common. Anyone who has ever built a house knows that even the best plans don't work out the way you think they will. But just because the process isn't foolproof, a solid plan that needs adjustment will always be a thousand times better than a general idea and flying by the seat of your pants.

Many people in the 1980s drank the communication Kool-Aid of "being honest with your feelings." At the time, this was pretty cutting-edge communication stuff. It was liberating to the oppressed and co-dependent. Finally, people felt like they had a voice, and they used it. Unfortunately, as liberating as it was, it was a titanic mistake in its attempt to improve communication and resolve conflict. Saying something to get it off your chest is not responsible or effective communication.

Some people get really annoyed when they think about being careful with what they say and how they say it. They think that being careful is "sugarcoating things." They believe if they think before they speak that they will dilute their message.

Saying something without really thinking about the response is much like building a house without a blueprint. Unless you don't care about the outcome, confronting your spouse without thinking about it will be just as disastrous as building a house without a blueprint.

A healthy marriage needs to have conversations addressing each other's particular preferences and needs.

There are going to be times in your marriage when you would like something different to happen. It's important to talk about those things. Contrary to popular belief, no matter how much a person loves their spouse they will not be able to read their mind. As a result conflict is going to happen. And if we want things to improve, we need to have these conversations. Conflict will be either constructive or destructive depending on how you handle it. To make conflict constructive and productive, use a blueprint. In other words, before you open your mouth and start putting words together, it's a good idea to think about what you want the outcome to be. Because if you are flying by the seat of your pants and winging it, chances are you are going to be very disappointed with the outcome.

Not thinking about how your criticism will be received is not only reckless communication but also demonstrates carelessness, selfishness, and inconsideration towards your spouse. Recall the last time you were bugged by your spouse and confronted them with something that was bothering you. Even if you were soft in your approach and took ownership of your feelings, ask yourself if your spouse listened carefully to what you said and validated your perspective? Did they communicate understanding? Did they follow it up with a commitment to change? Did they thank you for bringing up your concern and give you a big fat kiss? Probably not. The usual approach of "being honest with your feelings" will cause a knee jerk reaction of defensiveness, justification, explanation, and rationalization. Which, of course, was probably not your goal. Unless your spouse has a brown belt in Communication Kung Fu, your spouse will get defensive even when you "helpfully" point out things that bother you or you want different.

My approach is time-tested, proven, and powerful. This approach respectfully walks past the walls of defensiveness like you are wearing Harry Potter's invisibility cloak. Your message that would normally get blocked is received with open ears, open heart, and open arms.

During a presentation a few years ago, one of the participants shared that he found that COMMUNICATING WITH THE DESIRED OUTCOME IN MIND was like exercising Jedi "mind powers." He was really excited. It blew him away that he could improve his influence by considering what he wanted the outcome to be and following this program. Understanding some basic psychological processes can help you put strategies together that not only enhance the likelihood of getting your DESIRED OUTCOME IN MIND but will also strengthen your relationships. In addition to improving the likelihood of getting what you want, the process itself is actually more respectful and honest than the old-fashioned "being honest with your feelings" program.

The primitive approach to confronting someone was to point out what you don't like when you are upset, miffed, bugged, offended, disappointed, or frustrated, and then tell the person what you would like them to do. As surprising as this might be, that actually isn't effective.

Instead of thinking about what you need to say when you are upset or want something to change, think about what you want the outcome to be. To start this process, imagine your were able to say everything you needed to say, and you said it perfectly. The conversation was like pure magic. Ask yourself what would you want the other person to think, feel, and do after you had this magical conversation? Don't think about what you would say. Just think about what your spouse would think, feel, or do once the magical conversation was over. If you don't know what you want the outcome to be, chances are you are just complaining. Once you figure out what you want the outcome to be, consider what your spouse would need to *see*, *hear*, or *experience* such that the outcome you want would likely be the natural response.

At the beginning of the chapter there was an interaction between Jen and Mike talking about going over the budget. Jen was getting frustrated and Mike was escaping to his room. Let's pretend Jen applied the principle of COMMUNICATING WITH THE DESIRED OUTCOME IN MIND with Mike.

First she identifies what she would like him to think, feel, and do. Jen would like Mike to *think* it is important for him to be involved in the family finances. She would like Mike to *feel* a sense of urgency in working on the family finances together. She would like him to *feel* a sense of appreciation for her making it important. Next, Jen identifies what she would like Mike to do. She would like Mike to listen carefully, sit down with her, and work on the budget. She would like him to be engaged and kind as they talk about the bills that need to be paid. She would like Mike to share what he would like their financial goals to be for the month. She would like Mike to take a more active role in taking care of the family finances on a monthly basis and show more initiative. She would love it if Mike would say that he appreciated her for getting him more involved.

After she has identified what she wants the desired outcome to be, the next step is to think about what Mike would need to *see*, *hear*, or *experience* in order to want to sit down with Jen and work on the budget and family finances. Notice what I said here. I didn't say she was to think about what she needs to *say* or *do*. Instead, she needs to think about what *he* would need to see, hear, or experience to actually want to make it a priority to sit down with Jen and work on their budget together.

Next to the gremlins that control thinking, everyone has a miniature replica of their spouse that lives in the back of their minds. The proof is that we can actually hear their voice from time to time when we consider things our spouse would have an opinion about. We can bounce ideas off of that miniature replica to see how the real spouse will react to things. When COMMUNICATING WITH THE DESIRED OUTCOME IN MIND, this miniature replica of your spouse is extremely valuable. We can actually have a conversation with this mini spouse to help us be more mindful of what they think and feel about things. When we tap into this special source of knowledge we are able to get inside their heads and figure out what they need to experience so we know what to say and do to get the desired outcome. This process involves using the principle DEFINING AND ACCEPTING REALITY.

Instead of Jen believing she should be able to say whatever comes to mind and have Mike magically understand and accept it, she identifies what *he* would need to see, hear, or experience such that he would want to do something different. She does this by consulting with the mini-Mike that lives in the back of her own mind[1]. This way she maximizes her influence by taking Mike's thoughts, feelings, and experiences into consideration. *Accepting reality* is manifest when Jen incorporates objective reality into how she would need to approach Mike. So Jen asks herself the following questions:

1. What would it take for Mike to think that it would be a good idea to sit down with Jen and work on the budget and family finances?

2. What would Mike have to see, hear, or experience for him to want to sit down and listen to her and work on the budget?

[1]When you consult with the mini replica of your spouse you don't make a value judgment. You just take what the miniature replica says at face value. You might find that the miniature spouse would like certain things that you aren't willing or able to do. That is OK Just because you may not agree with what the miniature spouse says, doesn't mean that we should discount it.

3. What would Mike need to see, hear, or experience in order for him to take the initiative of working on the budget with Jen?

4. Finally, what would he need to see, hear, or experience for him to feel a sense of appreciation for her taking the lead on something so important to their family's success?

If you get stuck trying to figure out what your spouse needs to see, hear or experience, try putting yourself in your spouse's shoes and answer the questions. Answering these questions will actually tell you what you need to say and do in order to get your desired outcome.

> Question: "What would Mike need to see, hear, or experience in order for him to understand how important it is for him to sit down with Jen and work on the budget?"
>
> Answer: Simply bringing up the topic of the budget will do that. The importance of the budget is actually communicated when Jen initiates a conversation about their family finances and the need to sit down and talk about it. This will naturally happen if she follows the steps in the process described in this chapter.
>
> Question: "What would Mike need to see, hear, or experience in order for him to *want*

to sit down with her and really figure things out?"

Answer: He would need to feel safe. He would probably need to feel some sense of understanding from her about why he might be so reluctant to work on the budget. In this particular case, as Jen consults with the miniature replica of Mike in the back of her mind, she realizes that he might feel like his opinion doesn't really matter or that if they create a budget, he will feel like she is controlling him. He might need to hear her say something about how in the past she has been stubborn and controlling about how their budget should be and that she realizes this tendency and wants to change. It also might help for him to hear that she can see how having a budget seems restrictive, especially since she keeps bringing up that they need to make changes with how they spend money.

Question: "What would Mike need to see, hear, or experience, so that Mike would initiate the monthly session regarding their budget and finances?"

Answer: As Jen consults the miniature Mike, she realizes that she needs to make sure that Mike feels really supported and comfortable. She also realizes that in order for Mike to take the lead, it may take a few months of him feeling like his opinions matter, and his ideas are important. The only thing she can think Mike would want to hear her say is that when he takes the lead she feels really secure in their financial situation and that makes her trust him and want to be more vulnerable and intimate with him[2].

QUESTION: "What would Mike need to see, hear, or experience in order for him to actually appreciate her taking the lead on something so important to their family's success?"

---

[2]Some women who read this may find this offensive as if there is a sexual reward if he will take more initiative or that sex is a bartering tool that is used to get him to do something. However, it isn't a reward at all. There are two factors at play here. First, consulting with the miniature spouse might reveal that bringing up the topic of sex naturally gets his attention. Second, as with the case of this scenario and many other women, it is very common for a woman to want to connect sexually when she feels supported and valued and that her needs are important. When a woman doesn't feel like her needs are important to her husband the wife is less likely to want to connect sexually. Men don't commonly think about the connection between emotional intimacy and sexual intimacy. When she gets his attention and makes the connection, she is being honest and clear in her communication in a way that he can understand.

> Answer: Mike would just need to feel understood, validated, and supported instead of feeling attacked. If they are able to have a good conversation about making these important decisions together and seeing how working together actually works, he will naturally appreciate it.

Sometimes I get people wondering if this process is really worth it. I hear "do I have to go through this whole process every single time I want to bring something up?" Maybe. If you really don't care about what the outcome is, then you can always wing it and hope for the best and see what happens. If you do care about what you want the outcome to be, then the process is important. I've identified some guidelines that will make this process run a lot smoother. The good news is that the process becomes first nature the more you do it. It becomes almost instantaneous. The more you practice, the easier it gets.

The more Jen thinks about it, the more she realizes how important it is to consider the issue of timing when she talks to Mike. She needs to think about when and how to have this conversation. She can't start talking to him while he is in the middle of watching a TV program or while he is on the computer. This is part of the "What would he need to experience?" component. As she thinks about it, she realizes that the best time to approach him would be after dinner when they are winding down for the night. Aside from what she might say, he might like her to sit by him and take his hand and apologize for being so controlling in the past. There may be more elements to consider, but the point is to really get in the head of the other person and think from their point of view about what they would need to see, hear, or experience in order to want to create the desired outcome in mind. This process of figuring out what they *need* to say is something that most people just skip past on their way to figuring out what they *want* to say.

Jen has identified the desired outcome. She has determined that Mike needs to be approached without attacking him. She also knows how and when to approach him that would likely result in him being more able to listen to her. All she has to do now is approach him the way she planned following the process of ASSUMING GOOD INTENT. If you recall in chapter 1, I mentioned that ASSUMING GOOD INTENT not only prevents you from getting hurt it is also a fantastic tool when you are going to confront someone. This is the situation where you get to use ASSUMING GOOD INTENT as a communication tool.

The approach that seems to be the most effective for increasing the likelihood of obtaining the desired outcome in mind follows a four-step approach. The first step involves telling the person what you think and feel about what is going on.

It might be easier to understand if I show you, then tell you. Let's see how all of these components work together in real life scenario where Jen approaches Mike about paying the bills and going over their budget. At the appointed time while they are winding down one evening, Jen initiates the conversation:

STEP 1: Telling the person what you think and feel about what is going on.

Jen: "I need to be honest with you about something that has really been bugging me. Every time I pay the bills and work on our family finances, I get so resentful that you never work with me on this that I just seethe inside."

STEP 2: The second step involves applying the principles of ASSUMING GOOD INTENT. In this scenario Jen is going to explain why Mike avoids helping with the fiancés and budget in a way that is compelling and kind.

Jen: "Over the past couple of days of stewing, I started thinking about why you avoid working on the budget with me. When I put myself in your shoes, I realize that I'm contributing to you not wanting to work on a budget with me. In the first place, I'm wrong in my assumption that you don't care. I believe that you really do care. But what is making it hard for you is that when we have done this in the past, I completely take over and try talking you into doing what I want to do instead of really giving your ideas a chance. Plus, I'm probably putting so much pressure on you about finances that it comes across that I think you are not a good provider. I don't know if that is totally it, but if I'm honest with myself, I can see that that's what I'm doing."

Step 3: The third step involves a quick "*Checking In*" type question to make sure you understand the situation correctly.

Jen: "Does that sum it up for you?"

Notice how Jen maneuvered the conversation from an attack to a sweet, loving understanding interaction by switching to ASSUMING GOOD INTENT. There is a social law at play here. When someone feels like the other person is trying to really understand there is no reason to become defensive. Even if Jen is wrong about her assumptions in the beginning, the attempt to make him a victim of circumstances rather than a villain is psychologically soothing. With his defenses down, Jen's message has been completely delivered. The message about working on the budget as something important to her has been delivered even though she didn't actually use the words: "It is important to me that we work on the family budget."

Feeling understood and respected, Mike can explain himself and expose the barriers that prevent him from wanting to work on the budget. Once these barriers are addressed and validated, the barriers are removed, and he is left with no more excuses. Mike can then respond:

> Mike: "You nailed it! I just figure that as long as I can avoid something that I already know is going to be painful, I might as well just deal with you being upset. So that's why I've avoided it. Also, I just get so stressed out about finances and feeling like a failure, I'd rather just let you figure things out and tell me what you want me to do because I don't really feel like I can do anything more than I'm already doing anyway."

Step 4: Finally, a request is made to actually resolve the issue.

> Jen: "So what would it take for you to want to sit with me and get this figured out?"

Notice how Jen completes step four after Mike reiterated the feelings of frustration he has had. This brings closure to the principle of communicating with the desired outcome in mind. The way Jen approached the conversation helped her deliver the message that the budget was important to her. By the time they are done with the conversation, Mike is likely to feel a sense of appreciation for her taking the lead on this without her saying something like: "You should appreciate me for doing this because there are a lot of women out there who spend money they don't have and put their family in serious debt."

Communicating with the desired outcome in mind is the process of creating a powerful approach to maximize your influence in getting what you want. The messages have been delivered, and the tone is set for resolution. And although the process didn't actually make Mike jump up and down for joy, Mike and Jen are just moments away from making a plan to sit down together and make a budget. Jen was also able to recognize her role in preventing Mike from wanting to do the budget. This definitely wouldn't have happened if she followed the "be honest with your feelings"/"fly by the seat of your pants" program. Using this approach sets up an emotional environment where they can develop a budget they can both live with. And besides being able to work on the budget together, they did something more important. They bonded over what could have been another argument.

Let's apply this principle in another scenario. Let's say Jim wants to talk to Holly about their sexual relationship. He feels hurt that his wife isn't being physically affectionate and sexually responsive. Let's look at how a typical conversation might go.

Jim: "Hey Babe, last night I tried to initiate sex, and you pretty much shut me down. Again. I'm just a little upset that I have to do all the work in that department of our relationship and to be honest it isn't fair. I'd do anything to make sure your sexual needs are met and it doesn't seem like my needs are that important to you."

Holly: *(Gushing with emotion)* "Oh, Hun! I'm so sorry! You are right. You're doing so much of the work, and I'm taking advantage of that. How about I make it up to you tonight?"

If you think a wife would respond like this naturally on her own you must have a pet unicorn. Because in the real world, the more likely response from the wife would be:

Holly: "Well, the reason I shut you down was because you didn't even bother to help get me in the mood. You know I hate it when you just go right for it. It makes me so mad, I can't help but just shut down. It seems like when you want it you just go for it and I just have to be there for you."

Jim: "Why is it always me that has to get you in the mood? Why don't you take the initiative? Don't you think it should be about us? Why do you do that? Why do you

> make it that I'm being selfish? You are the one being selfish because I have to approach you perfectly before you even think about it. That's selfish."

Not only is the plane going down, but it just caught fire. We can easily see that this is not going in the direction he was hoping. If his intentions were to increase his wife's appreciation for him and increase her awareness of the importance of her taking more initiative in the bedroom, then it didn't go very well. If he thought that she would have a stronger desire to make sure his sexual needs were met, those hopes have gone up in smoke with the crash and burn.

> "A blatant complaint is a pathetic strategy to create change."

What if he decided to apply the principle of COMMUNICATING WITH THE DESIRED OUTCOME IN MIND? First, he would have to identify what he wants the outcome to be. That's simple. He wants Holly to take more initiative in the bedroom and be more sexually receptive. As Jim consults with the miniature replica of Holly that lives in the back of his mind, he realizes that in his particular case he really doesn't have to do much. All Holly wants is to feel special to him. She wants Jim to think about her and care about her when they aren't in the bedroom. The little voice in Jim's head asks him to imagine what might be different if he were to have followed a different approach and left a few voice mails or quick texts from work:

> Jim: *(at 10:00 AM from work)* "Honey, I've been thinking about how lucky I am to have you as a wife, and how hard you work to take care of the kids and the house and everything. I've just been thinking about you a lot lately and I just can't get you out of my mind."

At this point, Holly might just think something is seriously wrong with him, especially if this is outside his normal behavior. Even though she might catch on to what Jim is up to, she may not even care. Hearing this from Jim is so emotionally warming, she can't help but start to melt[3].

> Jim: *(1:00 PM from work, right after lunch)* "I have been daydreaming about you all morning. Man I miss you! I think I'm going to have a hard time keeping my hands off of you when I come home."

[3]Each couple is different. The important concept to take home is the importance of addressing what your *spouse* needs to see, hear, or experience. Getting into your spouse's head and heart is what causes an emotional and psychological shift into being mindful of the other person. This is the essence of a healthy marriage. With a shifted attitude, the behavior changes will be much easier.

Jim: *(4:45 PM)* "Hey babe, I'm just wrapping things up at work. Is there anything you need me to pick up on my way home to make your evening go a little better?"

In addition to communicating his interest in her, the miniature replica of Holly tells him he needs to touch her in non-erogenous zones in order to get her body to be receptive to being touched in her erogenous zones. This isn't a guarantee. She may have had a bad day. She may be experiencing PMS. There may be other factors, but if Jim really considered what Holly needed, the likelihood of getting a desired outcome with this approach is substantially increased. It is respectful and responsible. What is more important, even if Jim's motives were a little selfish, the effort of going through this process provides the pathway for Jim to become more selfless. It is the process of developing a sense of mindfulness that creates the change.

Another example of the wrong way:

Husband: *(In an irritated & hostile tone)* "I know you have a thing for the karate instructor! I'm not blind. You don't think I see how he looks at you and talks with you and how you just smile and soak it all in? I want the kids pulled out right now! If you think I'm going to pay to have some sneaky weasel teach my kids karate while trying to break up our marriage and ruin our family, you're crazy!"

Wife: "Oh, I'm so sorry! You're right! I feel terrible about leading him on by not telling him to not flirt with me. What can I do to prove my love is only for you?"

Time out! Really? I just needed to make the point again how ridiculous we are when we share our unfiltered, honest feelings thinking that it *should* bring about the change we want. If you think this is a likely outcome, you probably have fairies that play with your pet unicorn. The more likely response would be:

Wife: "Are you kidding me? I can't believe you are accusing me of wanting something with the karate instructor. So what if he flirts with me? Just because I'm not mean and rude to him doesn't mean I have a thing for him. You know what the problem is? You're jealous. You have some serious insecurity problems. If you are going to accuse me of that, you need some serious help, because I haven't done anything wrong."

Notice how being honest with his feelings backfired? I don't think the husband realized that his approach was going to lead to this outcome. In fact, the motivation behind his attempt at being honest with his feelings was his wish that she would reassure him. But that is not going to happen—not when he approaches her with an accusation. When she gets wrongfully accused, she is not going to feel bad for how her husband feels. Nor is she going to feel a profound need to reassure him. She is going to feel insulted and indignant. That's true even if the accusation is founded and completely true.

Let's compare this scenario with how it might be different applying the principle of COMMUNICATING WITH THE DESIRED OUTCOME IN MIND:

First, the husband recognizes that he feels a strong sense of betrayal, and he's mad at his wife for not shutting down the karate instructor's flirtatious interaction. Second, he employs the principle of ASSUMING GOOD INTENT. Remember, when ASSUMING GOOD INTENT, he explains what happened with compelling reasons for why she didn't shut the karate instructor down. In ASSUMING GOOD INTENT, the husband will make sure his explanation follows the assumptions that 1) She didn't mean to hurt his feelings, 2) She wants him to feel good, and 3) She is doing the best she can. In this case he explains to himself that the reason she doesn't shut the karate instructor down is that she doesn't want to make things awkward with the karate instructor, especially since he does a great job with the kids and they really like him. The husband then combines this principle with the principle of DEFINING AND ACCEPTING REALITY. In *defining reality*, he realizes that the karate instructor flirts with all the good-looking moms, so she probably doesn't take it too personally.

Now that he has come up with a compelling believable reason for why she doesn't shut the karate instructor down, he identifies his desired outcome. He starts with the end in mind, as if he has already had a magical conversation and he got exactly what he wanted. How would he like her to think after the conversation? What would he like her to feel after the conversation? What would he like her to say or do after the conversation? In this situation, he wants her to understand that when she is friendly to flirtatious men that it makes him feel disrespected. He wants her to think that when she allows men to flirt with her it violates the security and safety of their marriage. He wants her to see how she hurt his feelings when she didn't make it clear that "karate boy's" flirt was not OK with her. He wants her to validate his feelings and work to find a solution to create better boundaries with the karate instructor and any other guy who flirts with her.

With an explanation from the principle of ASSUMING GOOD INTENT as to why she didn't shut the karate instructor down and a clear picture of what he wants the outcome to be, his next step is to consult the miniature replica of his wife that lives in the back of his mind about what she would need to see, hear, or experience in order to increase the likelihood of this desired outcome.

She needs to be approached in a non-accusing way, so she will be more receptive and less defensive. If the focus is more on *his* feelings and interpretation rather than an attack on *her* behavior, the message won't come off as an attack. Knowing his wife to shy away from super-serious conversations, he realizes that he doesn't need to make it über serious in order for her to know that he is serious.

With his preparations complete and the blueprints drawn, he is ready to bring up the issue. Let's see how putting this all together might sound. Put yourself in the wife's shoes and judge for yourself if the outcome of this scenario might seem reasonable and realistic.

> Husband: "Hey Babe, you know that karate instructor our kids go to."
>
> Wife: "Yeah."
>
> Husband: "I have a confession to make. When I noticed him putting his flirt on with you and you being all sweet and friendly, I started getting all jealous and mad. Mad that he's openly flirting with you and mad that you didn't do anything to stop him. I started feeling bad for myself that you were not defending our marriage. Truth is, I was really upset, but after thinking about it, I feel bad for thinking this way. I can see I was over-reacting and reading more into it than I should. I let my insecurities get the best of me. I hate to admit it but sometimes I worry I'm not enough for you, and that someday you will discover how much better

you can get and leave me. Especially someone that's way awesome and breaks boards with his bare hands. So, I'm sorry that I let my insecurities run away from me. I'm sure the reason you didn't shut him down or call him out on it was because you were just trying to be nice. Plus, it could have been a weird situation if you called him out for flirting with you. You don't want to make things awkward with the kids or with the other parents who were around. Even though, I have to admit that could be pretty interesting to see. But I guess what I'm trying to say is, I didn't realize how bad it bugged me until I saw you respond so friendly to his flirtatiousness as he flattered you and your eyes were all sparkly. I know I'm kinda selfish because I only want you to sparkle for me."

Wife: "Oh my gosh. He does that all the time. I thought since you were there tonight, he would stop. I just don't know what to do! I don't have a clue what I should do. If it were some random stranger, I would just blow him off and walk away or tell him to bug off. But the kid's karate instructor is someone I have to see and talk to all the time. What should I do?"

Assuming good intent is pure magic when confronting someone. It is a fantastic way to say what is on your mind when you are frustrated, disappointed, or just miffed without an attack. This component cannot be overstated because if your spouse feels attacked by what you are saying, then the game is over. You've lost. Once your spouse feels attacked, they put their energy into self-preservation and self-justification rather than validation and reconciliation.

Communicating with the desired outcome in mind isn't the way we naturally think. Getting and staying physically fit isn't something that comes natural either. Success in life is the process of identifying the laws that govern success and then living them. Swinging a tennis racquet or a golf club the *wrong* way may feel really natural. When a trainer teaches you how to do it *correctly*, it might feel very awkward in comparison. But with practice, it will soon become first nature and what once was mechanical and forced will be effortless and easy.

Step 1: Identify what you want the outcome to be.

Step 2: Consult with the mini-replica of your spouse to identify what your spouse needs to see, hear, or experience in order for the outcome to be natural.

Step 3: Execute:

- Share how and why you got upset.

- Shift into assuming good intent by saying something like "But then I realized," or "After thinking about it... I wasn't being fair." Then explain the situation assuming good intent. Explain why he/she did or didn't do what you wanted them to in a positive and understanding manner.
- Take responsibility for your role in the situation. Perhaps lack of communication, or being overly sensitive, not understanding the situation etc.
- Finish by sharing what you hope the outcome of the conversation would be[4].

Communicating with the desired outcome in mind directs your thoughts and feelings towards the thoughts and feelings of your spouse. You become more understanding and patient. The very process of bringing up an issue compels you to think of your spouse's feelings and perspectives. The process brings you closer together and creates greater mutual understanding. Take your time. Start out slowly. Go through each of the steps

[4]You can actually go through the bullet points of your list of what you want the outcome to be. You can start with "I was just hoping that after we talked, you would know how important this is to me, and that you would recognize how hurt I get when this happens. I was hoping that after our conversation that you would work with me to figure something out."

over and over until the process becomes more comfortable. If you skip any of the steps, you will run the risk of not getting the results you want and you might miss the opportunity to experience greater closeness.

Manipulation vs. Communicating with the Desired Outcome in Mind

The difference between being manipulative and COMMUNICATING WITH THE DESIRED OUTCOME IN MIND is that the first has an element of dishonesty and disrespect and selfishness while COMMUNICATING WITH THE DESIRED OUTCOME IN MIND is honest and respectful. Manipulation violates the other person by using what you know about them to get what you want regardless of what's in their best interest. COMMUNICATING WITH THE DESIRED OUTCOME IN MIND, takes into consideration what is in your spouse's best interest. A lasting intimate relationship will be weakened when manipulation is present.

COMMUNICATING WITH THE DESIRED OUTCOME IN MIND is a respectful, responsible communication process that shows awareness of your spouse's wants and needs in a true sense of unconditional love. It not only requires a deeper sense of knowing your spouse, it facilitates it. It requires and develops a great deal of self-discipline. Practicing this principle over and over helps develop the kind of qualities and attributes of integrity that create long lasting trust, friendship, and emotional intimacy.

The power that comes through in your communication does not come from the volume of your voice, but in the heart felt sincerity and sensitivity of what you say. The next chapter breaks down the power of communication into their smaller components so you will understand how to say what you need to say to maximize your influence in creating greater closeness and getting what you want.

Chapter 4

Clear, Direct, and Sensitive Communication

> Kind words are a creative force, a power that concurs in the building up of all that is good, and energy that showers blessings upon the world.
>
> LAWRENCE G. LOVASIK

Tommy is sitting at the dinner table, laptop open, clicking away at keys. Megan, his wife, is starting the dishes. As Megan gets the water going, she looks over at Tommy and asks for help with the dishes. "I wish I had time to do the things that I'd like to do tonight." In Megan's mind, the message was clear, but Tommy doesn't stir. However, when Megan starts moving the pots and pans more aggressively an icy breeze floats past Tommy, and he looks up from his computer with a completely bewildered and confused look on his face.

Have you ever wondered why people communicate the way they do? I compare the way people communicate much like artists paint. If you are familiar with abstract paintings like those of Jackson Pollock, you realize that sometimes the artists' intentions are designed to communicate a feeling or mood rather than accurately depict any particular person or place. This is very different from the works of realists like Goustav, Courbet, and Norman Rockwell. Realists try to capture every wrinkle in a person's skin or impart the texture of tree bark so you could almost feel it just by looking at the painting.

Much like the realists use deliberate brush strokes to capture every detail they see, some people are very deliberate in the words they use. They try to stay as true to reality as they can. They value objectivity in evaluating events and facts as they remember them. They say what they mean, and they mean what they say. Sometimes they get right to the point. "Why sugarcoat the truth?" is their rationalized rhetoric. "Say what you mean and mean what you say." "If they get offended, that's their problem."

Some people communicate more abstractly. They

may use broad strokes—overgeneralizing, hinting, exaggerating, or talking around subjects. The message they send is more than the actual meaning of the combinations of words they use. They may exclaim, "Don't get hung up on the words I use. Listen to what I'm trying to say." They don't have a strong devotion to remain true to the objective facts as much as they attempt to be true to the feelings or ideas they have. The words they use may not actually mean what they are trying to say. For emotional communicators, words are used like an impressionist's paint brush—for expression.

When these people say something like: "Why don't you care about me?" or "You never show me that you love me." They don't actually mean what they say. The communication decoder ring (that actually doesn't come included with the marriage packet) could translate this message as one of a hundred different interpretations based on the context of the statement. It could be translated as: "She doesn't feel like he is making her a priority." It could also be interpreted as, "She doesn't feel like they are really connected." It could be that *he* hasn't initiated sex or a back rub in a while. It could also be that *he* is forgetful and doesn't make holidays a big deal like she would like. Passive aggressive statements are made almost unconsciously. Sometimes they hint at things rather than address them directly.

Are these types of communication effective? Absolutely not! But to a lesser or greater degree, we all do it. We do it because that's how our parents did it. It seems natural and it happens effortlessly. It's how we learned to communicate. We do it because we have not been trained how to do it differently. How would we know any differently? We don't learn this stuff in school. Heaven forbid we spend time working on social interactions that actually matter in life instead of learning a foreign language where over 90% of the students enrolled will never speak the language outside the classroom. Did I mention world geography?

As we explore how to communicate more effectively, I have identified three components: *Clear*, *Direct*, and *Sensitive*. To illustrate these components, I will use our married couple Tommy and Megan. While the kids are watching television, Tommy is sitting at the kitchen table with his laptop computer open. Megan is doing the dishes at the sink. Megan would like some help doing the dishes, so she can read the last few chapters of her book before she goes to bed. Megan will ask Tommy to help with the dishes four different ways. The first way will be unclear and indirect. The second will be clear but indirect. The third will be clear and direct but not very sensitive Finally, the fourth will be clear, direct, and sensitive.

Pay carefully attention to the different ways Megan asks, and think about whether you are familiar with any of these styles. See for yourself if there is a natural emotional response to each of the styles. First, Megan asks Tommy to help with dishes in an unclear and indirect manner.

> Megan: "It would sure be nice if I had time doing something I'd like to do tonight."

This type of communication lacks all three components. First, it isn't really clear what she is asking. Unless you have been trained to interpret hints or can read minds, the statement she makes is more a vague declaration about how she feels about the situation, than a request for help. Second, it isn't direct. In other words, she hasn't specifically addressed Tommy. The tone of her martyrdom implies being victimized by Tommy, which is a guilt trip to get him to help. It assumes that in order to get his assistance to help, she needs to make him feel bad about not helping. This unclear and indirect approach is manipulative and insensitive. Being passive with a soft tone doesn't actually make it kind. Even if Tommy catches what she says and interprets it accurately, it doesn't change the fact that her communication is disrespectful and irresponsible.

Here is Megan's second attempt:

> Megan: "It would sure be nice if I could get some help doing these dishes."

In this attempt, Megan is clear in her communication about what she wants: help with the dishes. But the message is indirect. In other words, the request is not directed toward any particular individual. It is an assumption. This has the potential to work in some cases, but it is especially problematic if there are more than three people in the same room. Strictly speaking, Megan's request is really a declaration of her feelings than a request for help. Although her statement is more specific than her previous general declaration, it is still a declaration. Megan fails to get Tommy's attention while she drops the hint. Indirect communication is manipulative. She is pretty clear about what she wants, but she is not directing her message toward *who* she is talking to. The risk is that Tommy may become offended by the very nature of *how* the message was delivered.

Now compare this to something clear and direct but not very sensitive.

> Megan: *(In a frustrated tone)* "Hey Tommy! Do you think you can turn off your computer for just ten minutes and help me with these dishes!?"

This request is very clear and very direct, but it lacks sensitivity. This version is blatantly disrespectful. It's easy to see how she has violated both ASSUMING GOOD INTENT and COMMUNICATING WITH THE DESIRED OUTCOME IN MIND. First, it assumes that he wouldn't be willing to help her. Also she assumes she needs to be abrupt to get his attention. Second, she hasn't considered what he would need to see, hear, or experience in order for him to *want* to help with the dishes.

After being approached like this, instead of Tommy being willing to help, he might feel attacked. If he is like most husbands, he might think that she was being rude. The "best case" scenario might be Tommy's compliance, but it might come with the price of resentment. What a miserable way to end the day. Even if he is a little dense, like some husbands are, being abrupt or insensitive doesn't actually increase his eagerness to help. Also, even if her tone was soft and pleasant sounding, the words she used didn't match her tone. This incongruence adds to confusion.

Now let's listen in as Megan works her magic with clear, direct, and sensitive communication. First, she will assume that he will be happy to help if he can. Second, she will accept the reality that in order for him to really listen to her request, she will need to get his attention. (Some guys, if their attention is on something, they are almost deaf.) And third, she asks in a way that will increase the likelihood of getting her desired outcome.

> Megan: "Hey Tommy," *(waiting for a response)* "I know that you are busy working on something, but would you mind helping me finish these dishes? If you would bring all the dirty dishes to me and then put away the ones I've already washed, it would really help. I have a few more chapters in my book I wanted to get through before going

> to bed tonight. Do you think you can give me a hand, Babe?"

When Megan asks in this manner, Tommy is able to step back from what he is doing and actually hear what she is saying. She doesn't have to resort to making any promises she doesn't intend to keep to motivate him either. When Megan is sensitive and speaks in a kind tone, there is no reason for Tommy to become defensive. He feels respected and appreciated. When he is treated like this, he may be more likely to please Megan and respond positively to her request, even if he is working on something really important. If for some legitimate reason Tommy isn't able to help, although disappointed, Megan can accept reality and finish the dishes on her own without criticism or complaint.

Notice how she takes into account ASSUMING GOOD INTENT by assuming Tommy would help if he could. This type of interaction sends a message of trust and confidence. Even if she is wrong, assuming that he would be willing to help if he could, increases the likelihood of a positive outcome[1]. She is also applying the principle of Accepting Reality. She accepts the reality that she needs to get his attention in order to make sure that he hears her. And third, she applies COMMUNICATING WITH THE DESIRED OUTCOME IN MIND when she considers what

[1] If the spouse has no interest in helping and expects her to do the dishes because it's "her job" or some other reason, refer to chapter 2.

Tommy needs to see, hear, or experience, including in this scenario a kind tone and an explanation for why she is asking him to help.

Communicating clearly, directly, and sensitively is not a strategy you can force by using the right words and trying to use the right tone. It is the result of really putting your spouse's interest and intents to the forefront of your mind. It is the result of ASSUMING GOOD INTENT, ACCEPTING REALITY, and COMMUNICATING WITH THE DESIRED OUTCOME IN MIND. Going against the natural tendency to motivate through manipulation, and instead look for the best in your spouse, is a deeper kind of love. This kind of love makes an individual stronger and a relationship closer.

To illustrate this even more, let's give Tommy a try with CLEAR, DIRECT, AND SENSITIVE COMMUNICATION. Imagine we continue with the previous scenario and Tommy gets up to help Megan do the dishes, but then the phone rings. Megan answers the phone and then walks out of the kitchen into the living room to talk, leaving Tommy to do the dishes on his own.

Imagine how Tommy might feel after being left to do the dishes by himself. Perhaps he thinks he got suckered. Imagine what Tommy might say if instead of applying the principles of CLEAR, DIRECT, AND SENSITIVE COMMUNICATION he applied another common communication program called the "I Feel… When You… Because" program.

(Megan just finishes the phone call as Tommy walks

in after doing the dishes.)

> Tommy: "Honey, can I talk to you? I feel hurt and betrayed. Because, when you asked me to help you with the dishes, I thought you meant "help." I didn't think it was fair for you to ask me to help and then bail on me when you got the first chance, and leave me to do the dishes by myself."

The chance of Tommy getting a heartfelt apology from Megan with this strategy is close to zero. Especially if he is unable to mask the slight sarcastic tone in his message, or his words are too measured and forced. If she is like most people, she is more likely to respond with:

> Megan: "Are you kidding me? You end up doing the dishes one time this week and you're seriously going to complain about it?"

This will not go well! And as foolish as this dialogue sounds, I'm not making this stuff up. It happens all the time where people get hurt feelings over the smallest things, and the flame of frustration and hurt start burning the relationship. This is why "clear, direct, and sensitive communication" is so important. It's a quick way to check yourself before you start talking. So let's pretend Tommy has figured this out and is going to be clear, direct, and sensitive. He may say something like:

> Tommy: "Hey Meg, after you took the phone call, leaving me to do the dishes by myself, I started getting upset with you, and then I caught myself feeling sorry for myself." *(So far he has applied Accepting Reality and is starting on the path of* ASSUMING GOOD INTENT.*)* "Then I realized that you probably wouldn't have taken the call if it hadn't been important. Is everything OK?" *(Now showing concern for the other person.)*

Notice, he isn't perfect. He admits he was upset. It's pretty understandable that this situation might result in a little bit of a "poor me" attitude. But by applying the principles and practices of CLEAR, DIRECT, AND SENSITIVE COMMUNICATION he was able to pull out of the communication death spiral.

CLEAR, DIRECT, AND SENSITIVE COMMUNICATION is a vital component to productive communication during times of stress and conflict. Using these principles as anchors or "check-points" in your communication is a way to ensure that when you communicate, you do it in a way that reduces confusion and misunderstanding. As you employ this principle you capture more power in your communication to strengthen your connection and work through the issues that could ruin your masterpiece of relational bliss.

Wouldn't life be great if we could all approach each other with these four communication commitments? It would be almost impossible to get offended. How could we be hurt and reactive when we are approached with such sensitivity, respect and kindness? Unfortunately we have to live in the real world. And in the real world more often than not, these important communication components are not only forgotten, most people don't even know they exist. People are going to be frustrated, rude, angry, and hurtful. Conflict will happen, and it will get spicy. Most people will melt down when the heat runs high. The next section will teach you how to maintain cool, calm, and collected confidence and composure in emotional flare-ups.

Chapter 5

Killing Criticisms

> Agree with thine adversary quickly, whiles thou art in the way with him.
>
> MATTHEW 5:25

Keanu Reeves plays a character named Neo in the hit movie *The Matrix*. In one scene the bad guys start shooting at him, and he is able to move so fast that it looks like the bullets are going in slow motion. He is able to dodge every bullet. Criticisms are like bullets. When they hit, they can really hurt. What if there was a way we could dodge mean words like Neo dodges bullets? You can.

Criticisms are a catalyst for conflict. Dale Carnegie in his book *How to Win Friends and Influence People* states that there are three C's we need to avoid. Those three C's are never *criticize*, *condemn*, and *complain*. Unfortunately, in spite of Dale Carnegie's efforts, the three C's are still alive. I want to teach people how to "Kill Criticisms." I'm talking about all criticisms, especially the ones intended to hurt.

A master of Kung Fu takes the force of the attack of the other person and channels it or turns the energy of the attack in a safe direction to protect the self and prevent harm. So instead of trying to block a punch, the energy of the punch is redirected. In communication, the most difficult relational situations have to do with responding to verbal attacks. It became apparent to me that no book on communication would be complete without a solid strategy to deal with critical comments, accusations, and allegations. Not in a blocking way, but in a redirecting way. Blocking might stop the criticisms but it won't create closeness. What we needed was some serious communication Kung Fu moves to deal with or handle inevitable verbal attacks.

Why do people say mean things? There are times when, in spite of our best intentions, our natural reactions to situations can get to our emotions before our minds catch up. Sometimes we get angry. Sometimes when we feel betrayed, disrespected, unimportant, feelings of insecurity, hurt, or frustration can cause our communication to come out a little spicy. This is called an emotional reaction. We don't intend to be mean and hurtful, it's just that we are so frustrated, tired, or, in my case hungry, that it just comes out with a sharp edge. It is during these times that conflict can become ugly and unproductive. I know when I'm critical, it's been when I don't feel appreciated or cared about. I feel sorry for myself and then feel justified in pointing out what my wife is doing or isn't doing that upsets me. Sometimes I get angry. I'm not saying being critical is OK; It's not. I'm saying that even when we are doing the best we can, there are going to be times when we will be critical. And as we learned in chapter 2, if we can predict, we better prepare.

Several years ago I read Manuel Smith's book *When I Say No, I Feel Guilty*. There is a part in his book where he teaches a strategy, he calls "fogging" to deal with criticisms. It was a cheeky way to dodge criticisms and create emotional distance from a person's verbal attack. His strategy was great if you didn't care about maintaining a relationship with the person being critical. In marriage we are going to experience times when our spouse is going to say something mean and critical. It's not that our spouses have succumbed to Satan, it's just part of being human. I expanded Manuel Smith's strategy of "fogging" and developed a process that would redirect criticism and create greater closeness instead of dodging it and creating distance.

To better help me explain the process of KILLING CRITICISMS, I will compare it to the process of panning for gold. When panning for gold, a large scoop of mud and water is dumped into the miner's pan. The miner who is panning for gold swirls the mud and water in the pan letting the top of the mud and water dump out with each swirl of the pan. Gold, the heavier material, finds its way to the bottom of the pan. This process continues as more water is added. With each gentle swirl, the mud and excess water is dumped out until gleaming in the bottom of the pan are the precious nuggets of gold. There is no focus or value in the mud, dirt, and rocks. The focus in on the gold. Even the fine gold powder is extremely valuable. Imagine that the scoop of mud, dirt, and rocks is the critical statement or allegation from your spouse. The golden nuggets or gold dust are the elements of truth in the criticism. When you think KILLING CRITICISMS, think panning. But instead of panning for gold, you are panning for the elements of truth.

The uneducated way to respond to criticism is to point out how the criticism isn't true or fair. The idea is to defend yourself or standup for yourself by pointing out how there are errors in your spouse's perception. No matter how much truth there may be in the criticism, we think that if we can point out how part of the criticism isn't fair or justified, we can protect ourselves from our spouse's malicious behavior. I've watched hundreds, if not thousands of couples deal with criticism. Being defensive rarely if ever gets the critical person to say, "Gee, you are right. I wasn't being fair when I said that mean thing to you was I?" More often than not the person who was being critical becomes more agitated and aggravated. This definitely doesn't increase the spouse's ability to be rational and reasonable. No matter how right you are, pointing out how a criticism isn't fair or right is a defensive response, and it doesn't work. No matter how natural it may be to respond to a criticism defensively, it will only create more tension and frustration, which actually keeps the criticism alive instead of *killing it.*

So how should you respond to criticisms? All criticisms will have an element of truth ranging from 0% (totally untrue) to 100% (totally true). The goal to KILLING CRITICISM is to listen for and respond *only* to the element of truth. Nothing more. Nothing less. After a criticism has been stated, really search inside yourself as if you had a Star Trek truth-seeker wand. See if you can acknowledge *any* truth to the criticism. You want to acknowledge as much as you can, so really search. This is not the normal response. As you search through your soul to find the golden nuggets of truth to the criticism, you will be able to sense the amount of truth in the criticism. Perhaps the criticism is totally true. Perhaps there may be more truth than you would like to admit but it isn't 100% true. Perhaps the person being critical has extremely exaggerated the issue and maybe there is only 5% truth to the criticism. Sometimes there may be no truth to the criticism at all. Sometimes the criticism is so unclear and ambiguous it's impossible to determine how much truth there is.

Let's take the criticism, "You never help around the house." If the criticism is 100% true, then the appropriate response would be to completely acknowledging how true the criticism is. For example you might say, "You are absolutely right, I don't do anything in the house to help out." Very rarely will any criticisms be 100% true, but if it is 100% true, then accept it, acknowledge it, and admit it. But if it is not 100% true and yet there is a great deal of truth to it, you might say, "You are right. I *don't do much* to help out around the house." There may be reasons why you don't do very much if anything *around* the house, but now is not the time to bring it up. The next chapter will go into detail on how you can explain yourself and address the part of the criticism that isn't true. Right now we are just focusing on agreeing with the part that *is* true, which is how we "kill it."

If the criticism is around 50% true, agree with as much truth as you can. You might say something like, "I don't do much around the house, I could do more. I could at least help out with cleaning the dishes after dinner instead of sitting on the couch." Agree to whatever part of the criticism you can.

What if there is only a fragrance of truth in the criticism or if your spouse really believes there is more truth than you can see? Agree with the *fragrance* of truth. Say something like "I can see that it *might appear* like I don't help out very much around the house." Be careful not to just say this to say it. You need to own it. Be able and willing to explain how it only *appears* you don't help out around the house. Notice, by focusing on what is true about the criticism, you point out what isn't true. In this scenario the spouse only accepted the truth that it only *appears like* he doesn't help around the house. He didn't say anything about why the criticism wasn't true. Yet, the confession that it only *appears* he doesn't help clearly communicates he doesn't agree with the criticism. Carefully acknowledging the element of truth is a pretty cool way of disagreeing without being disagreeable.

What if the criticism has 0% truth? What do you do then? You can say, "Yes I do! I help out all the time!" Stop right there! I was just testing you to see if you were paying attention. It is so tempting to point out how the criticism isn't fair or even true, especially if you don't see any truth at all. But I'm telling you, no matter how right you are, if you get defensive, your ship is going down. If your spouse makes a criticism and there is zero truth to it, or if it's ambiguous and vague, instead of getting defensive ask, "What do you mean?" This forces your spouse to reconsider what he/she is saying. When they respond with a more specific criticism, repeat the steps above by identifying what is true in the criticism and acknowledge it. When you ask, "What do you mean?" This will give you time to psychological "shift gears" and listen carefully, so you can sort through the mud for the golden nuggets of truth.

Refrain from making excuses or trying to explain yourself. Just stick with the truth of the statement. If you struggle to find any semblance of truth, and the critical person is adamant that there is truth, use the ace in your back pocket: "Perhaps from your perspective it might look like that." And if you say this, be prepared to back it up. This validates your spouse's perspective without agreeing with a criticism you don't agree with. Remember to really say it like you mean it. If it comes out sarcastic, you are getting defensive. If you say it and you don't mean it, you will be caught trying to avoid accountability.

Minimizing vs. Maximizing

When you search your soul for the nuggets of truth, make sure you maximize the truth instead of minimizing it. If you minimize the truth of the criticism, you will come across defensive. If you minimize, your spouse will maximize. For example, let's say Johnny is making cookies one evening and Jennifer walks into the kitchen. Jennifer says something critical.

> Jennifer: "Ugh! You're making cookies again? You never clean up after yourself when you make cookies."

If the truth is more like 75% and Johnny responds by minimizing it, he will be throwing gas on a fire.

> Johnny: "Yeah, you are right. *Sometimes* I don't clean up after myself all the way."
> Jennifer: "Are you kidding? When have you *ever* cleaned up after yourself?

You can see that Johnny would be much better served if he just acknowledged that his wife was more right than he'd like to admit.

As we have discussed earlier, people are going to be hurtful and rude. They do it when they are angry. They do it when they feel hurt, insecure, or frustrated. At this moment, there is no use in trying to be logical. When a person is really upset because they are hurt, insecure, frustrated, or angry, it is very difficult to listen. It's actually not even a choice, it's a chemical inability of the mind. The more upset a person is, the more emotional and less reasonable they become. Even if the critical person isn't emotionally upset to the point of losing reason, why would they listen to someone if they don't feel their spouse has their best interest at heart? Even when there is a completely rational explanation, people will struggle to really listen if they don't feel cared for. If you are wondering when to explain yourself or point out when the other person is wrong, there will be a time, but not yet. Right now, the only thing you need to focus on is searching through the mud to find the golden nuggets of truth. Your job, if you do it well, will be to agree with as much truth as you can. Because if you minimize, your spouse will maximize.

This is a good time to reiterate the importance of being real with your feelings. Agreeing with the element of truth isn't just saying the words. It's feeling it first, and then using words to describe the feelings. Let's illustrate. The phrase, "you're absolutely right" could mean a variety of things based on the tone, volume, pace of words, facial expression, and body language. I have separated these variations into five levels of emotional intensity. The first one I call *emotional paragliding* because it is far from connecting any emotional sensitivity to the words. Although the words are saying, "You're absolutely right"; the tone, volume, pace, etc. is saying "I don't care... take a hike." The second level of emotional intensity, I compare to *water skiing*. In emotional water skiing, we are just skimming the surface of emotional connectedness. The message is, "So you have a point, so what?" The third level is *snorkeling*. In this level there is more sensitivity, but it lacks depth and conviction. The message is very matter of fact, "OK, you are right, what is the point in talking about it. I said you're right. Let's be done with it." The fourth level of emotional intensity is *scuba*. In *scuba* level, we are attaching emotion with the words. At this level, there is a sense of understanding of the other person's experience and how the relationship is affected. It's saying, "I understand; I'm hearing you." And finally, *deep sea diving*. The *deep sea diving* level of communication transforms words into an emotional experience. At the *deep sea diving* level, the individual captures the emotional essence to the core. There is not only a recognition of the statement, but a reverent empathic understanding expressed with emotion. It's not only saying, "I hear you." It's saying, "I feel you."

Here is an example of a conversation with a couple dealing with a criticism. In this scenario, Megan is upset with Tommy. Tommy has left his workout clothes in the bathroom a few days in a row. She is really upset. Although she understands the principles of good communication, she is tired and overwhelmed. She temporarily slips into old patterns of communication. It might sound something like this:

> Megan: *(In a frustrated, aggravated tone)* "Tom! You left your gym clothes on the bathroom floor again this morning! This is the third time in a row and I'm sick of it!"

I think you can imagine how Tommy would respond if he was not KILLING CRITICISM, and the result would be just as predictably awful. But if we include this lesson learned, it might look something like this:

> Tommy: *(Sincerely)* "You know, I hate to admit it, but you're absolutely right."

At this point, Megan will continue with another criticism, ask a question, make a declaration, give a lecture, or issue a command, but we will address those options in the next section. Right now all we want to do is deal with the critical statement. If Megan says something else that is critical, Tommy will listen for the element of truth and acknowledge it. Ultimately, Megan will run out of critical statements and shift into one of the other options.

I've found that a confident and contrite acknowledgement of a criticism can come as quite a surprise to the person being critical. As a result the critical person will feel heard and validated and soften quickly.

Of course, no one likes being on the receiving end of criticism. Be careful. Do not try to get out of being the target of a criticism too soon. An attempt to avoid being the target of criticisms, by quickly adding an explanation or excuse will come across being defensive. Imagine if Tommy said something like this:

> Tommy: "I hate to admit it, but you're absolutely right... It's just that I've been in a hurry each morning to get to work on time."

If Megan is upset about Tommy leaving his clothes on the bathroom floor, and Tommy responds with an acknowledgement followed by a quick excuse, she is going to be very put out. And if she was upset before she criticized Tommy, she will most likely get more upset at his pathetic excuse. It might go something like:

> Megan: "Come on Tommy, how much time does it take for you to pick up your clothes and put them in the hamper? What? 20 seconds? Maybe you should wake up 20 seconds earlier so you can make sure you have the time to put your clothes in the hamper."

This illustrates how important it is to avoid making excuses or giving reasons and explanations until the time is right. The next chapter will show you how and when to give your explanations. It will show you how you can point out the important misunderstandings of the critical spouse and give an explanation that might help them understand the situation better.

For now, when your spouse is critical, just respond to the element of truth. If there is a valid reason for why you did what you did, or at least an explanation, you will have a chance to say it in a way you will be heard.

To reiterate, when we respond only to the element of truth, by default we communicate indirectly the part of the critical statement that isn't true. For example, if Megan told Tommy that it was the third time in a row he hasn't put his gym clothes away, and it was actually twice, having Tommy disagree that it was only twice instead of three times would most likely not result in an apology from Megan. In this case, Tommy could respond to Megan's criticism, "It's been the third time this week!" with something like this:

> Tommy: "I know it's been at least twice, and the truth of the matter is, once is too many. I should be taking care of my stuff instead of having you do it."

Notice how Tommy can disagree with the part of the criticism that *isn't* true by being careful to acknowledge only what *is* true. When we agree with the part that is true, by default, we are disagreeing with the part that is not true. We do it, without actually saying it. Since the focus is on the element of truth, we can take charge of the interaction with composure and integrity. When people are critical in a rude and insensitive manner, they have temporarily lost their composure. Killing criticism tells your spouse that they don't have to be perfect to be heard and understood. When people feel heard and understood, they feel safe enough to open up and see things another way.

When someone says something critical, immediately say to yourself, "You know there is probably some truth to that." Then use your soul-searching scanner to identify as much truth as you can. If you need more time to do a full scan, you can say something like, "You know, let me think about what you just said. I feel like being defensive instead of really listening." This will buy you some time and help you search for the element of truth. Then go back to panning for truth. Pick out the parts of the criticism that you believe are true, and validate as many of the parts of the statement you can. If you can't identify any truth, or you're struggling to find the truth, say, "What do you mean by…?" This will slow the process down a bit so you can get your bearings.

Applying this strategy in a real life scenario can be a true challenge, especially when you are offended or feel attacked. Sometimes, just the idea of not being understood by the other person can contribute to a natural emotional reaction of defensiveness.

Be aware that there will be times when both spouses will get sucked into feeling hurt and offended during moments of miscommunication. It's part of being human. It is going to happen.

The application of these principles and strategies will diminish the frequency, intensity, and duration of the conflict when it happens. If you find yourself in one of these situations where you are both getting defensive, you can always say, "Hold on a second, I haven't been listening to you very well, I've been thinking about what I'm going to say. Will you say what you were saying again? This time I am going to try listening better." This will stop the downward spiral and help straighten things out a lot faster with less damage.

When you commit to principle-based responses like killing criticism, instead of passion-based reactions prompted by weakness and ignorance, you manifest strength of integrity and character. Anyone can be kind when they are treated kindly. It takes real character and strength to maintain principles of kindness when others are rude or hurtful.

Killing criticism is making your spouse a priority. It's accepting them as a real person with real struggles. It's a love that doesn't depend on the perfect approach. It is a love that is unconditional. Loving someone when they are not at their best is real love. It can't get more loving than that.

The next chapter walks you through all the components of conflict and how to deal with them. With the skills you will learn in the next chapter you can be confident in any situation where there is conflict.

Chapter 6

Fencing Conflict

> Swordplay is like conversation. You have to learn to listen to your opponent.
>
> FROM THE 1991 MOVIE
> "*By The Sword*"

When I was in high school, I attended a presentation and demonstration on the art of fencing.

The demonstrator explained that the long and flexible sword called a foil was designed by the French military to pierce through the chain links of the English soldiers' chainmail armor. I was mesmerized by the demonstration as I watched how the instructors slashed and clashed and stabbed and parried back and forth with wicked speed and Dartanyan confidence.

The desired effect was not lost on me. I was one of several handfuls of students who stayed after school for further instruction. We were taught five different attacks with the foil and five different parries to counter each of the attacks. The instructor gave special attention to teaching us the defensive movements and strategies called parries. He explained that untrained people when defending themselves have a tendency to wildly exaggerate their parry. These extreme defensive movements made them incredibly vulnerable to another attack. In other words, parrying one attack too aggressively put the person being attacked in a more vulnerable position than before the initial attack.

We learned that effective parries are actually small strategic movements that do just what is necessary to stay balanced, maintain position, and prevent injury. Once the five attacks and parries were mastered, we could slash and clash, stab and parry just like the Three Musketeers. In fact, after some practice, the person attacking could easily parry the attacker no matter the sequence of the five attacks.

Top right to bottom left … parry.

Right side … parry.

Left side … parry.

Lunge stab … parry.

Of course in real fencing, there are many more attacks than just the five basic ones we learned in the workshop after school. Fortunately, in communication, I have been able to identify that all relational conflict can be grouped into five basic categories, or "attacks." Understanding how to parry or respond to the five different moves will empower you to increase confidence, reduce conflict, and create closeness.

FENCING CONFLICT is not about creating a resolution or solving the problem. This might sound strange but trying to make the problem go away by solving it before mutual understanding takes place will not only result in a lousy solution but also will result in losing the opportunity for building trust and creating closeness.

The solution is less important than the process you used to get the solution. You never know if the solution you choose will actually work. In the next chapter, I will walk you through a process that helps resolve conflict and create closeness.

FENCING CONFLICT is a method for staying engaged in conflict where there is a person who is upset, angry, miffed, or frustrated. The tools and techniques you learn in this chapter will help you neutralize the intense emotions that inhibit reason, so you can talk[1].

The first objective in developing the skill of FENCING CONFLICT is learning how to recognize and categorize the five different "attacks."

1. Personal Criticism: A statement about your char-

[1] As a special side note, these simple strategies have become very popular with special interest groups that are dealing with abusive individuals and narcissists.

acter or your behavior.

2. Event Criticism: A statement about an event.

3. Declaration: A statement about themselves or a general statement about the situation.

4. Command: A statement telling you to do something.

5. Question: A statement requesting information.

There is one more component to this strategy that we will explore later called the Rest or The Pause. This is the moment of silence for a constructive counter move. It is the moment you have a chance to disagree and/or explain yourself. This will be explained in detail later in the chapter.

We will now break down each of the five components of conflict, and how to recognize and parry them.

Parry Criticisms: Agree with the element of truth

As a brief reminder, a personal criticism is a statement about a person's character or behavior. For example, the statement, "You are selfish and inconsiderate," is a critical statement attacking a person's character. "It was your fault we were late to the party" is a criticism attacking your behavior.

An event criticism is a statement about an event or situation. "It was really rude of your mom to completely ignore me when I was trying to talk with her." "Your coat does not belong on the floor; it belongs in the mudroom on its hook." These are examples of statements that are criticisms about an event or situation.

Criticisms can be disguised in the form of manipulative questions that aren't really questions at all. "Why do you always dramatize and overreact every time you get upset?" or "How can you continue living your life day after day harboring so much anger and resentment?" You can see that although the statement is worded in the form of a question, it is loaded with accusations and assumptions. It's a statement that really isn't a request for information. Criticisms can be non-verbal such as an eye roll that says, "You are such an idiot." Criticisms can also be embedded in sarcastic comments. Consider the following: "Thanks a lot for making sure you said good bye this morning!" when you forgot the good-bye kiss. Or "I'm glad you're feeling better." When in reality, you're not feeling better.

There is often an associated feeling of hurt when being criticized. Careful listening can help you identify the criticisms embedded in passive aggressive statements or criticisms embedded in questions. If you feel attacked, chances are, you have been criticized. If you aren't sure what the specific criticism is, no problem, just ask for clarification.

Once you have identified a critical statement just follow the steps you learned in the previous chapter. Identify the element of truth and validate the part that is true. Don't point out what isn't true. Stick with what is true. If there is no truth to the criticism just ask, "What do you mean?" Use words and phrases as a tool to measure the amount of truth to statements much like you would use measuring cups or socket sizes. If the criticism is 100% true, you can say words like "Absolutely Right." "I do that all the time." If it isn't quite 100% true, say, "I do that more than I realize." "Most of time that is what I do." "I hate to admit it, but I do that more often than not." If there is maybe 50% truth say, "Sometimes I do that." "I do that more than I should." "Man I have a real problem with that." If there is less truth than that say, "In the past that has been true." "There are times when I do that." If there is even less truth than that say, "I can see how it might come across like (look like, appear like, sound like, etc.) I do" or "From your perspective I do that." (Of course you would tailor these phrases so they actually made sense in your situation[2]. Right?)

If the criticism is in the form of a question and you aren't sure how to respond, you can either treat it as a criticism or as a question (We will discuss responding

[2]It might be especially helpful to explore different phrases to capture the amount of truth to a particular statement. You can go to EmilHarker.com and download the workbook to practice these principles and skills so you will be ready when it is time to use them.

to a question later). You can decide. Don't worry, if you choose to respond to a question as if it were a criticism and it really was a question, they will assure you that they were actually asking a question. Remember that just because you parry a criticism doesn't mean the person will automatically stop criticizing you. Be ready for another one. If a successful response to a criticism brings up another criticism, continue fencing the criticisms by acknowledging the truth in the criticism. You keep doing this until the person runs out of criticisms and switches to another attack, or rests.

If you are experiencing this kind of emotional dump, then congratulations! You have made a serious and positive impact on your relationship. Even if the topic of the criticism is about how awful you've been for the past 15 years, the process of really listening and validating your partner's frustrations can create a paradoxical bonding moment. In your spouse's eagerness to be heard, don't be surprised if your spouse goes through the file cabinets of every frustrating, hurtful thing you've ever done, especially if there is a lot of truth to the criticisms. The good news is you only have to do this a couple of times to validate your spouse and really send the message that you are completely listening. If this happens to you, don't get offended. You should celebrate it! They are finally in a position where they can let the past go! When a person's purged files of criticisms are validated, the criticisms lose their usefulness for future arguments. When you validate a criticism it's as if you are "cashing the check." Once the check is cashed, it loses its value and can't be cashed in again. When a person's frustrations and hurts are validated it doesn't make sense to keep holding on to them. With their hurts, frustrations and disappointments validated, they can *start* to "let go" of the resentment. Notice the emphasis on "start." Now he/she can be warmer, kinder, and closer as you develop lasting intimacy. If there are a lot of criticisms with a lot of truth to the criticism, then let's face it. You probably deserve it.

Imagine how such a conversation might sound:

Karl: "Look Jen, when you change plans with me at the last minute to be with your friends, I feel like you don't really love me."

Jen: "I can see how it would come across like that, especially since I have done that a few times recently."

Karl: "Yeah! You do it all the time and you don't even stop to think how rejected I feel! You go hang out with your friends, and I stay home wondering why you would rather be with them instead of me."

Jen: "You are right. I can see how you would feel bad when I bail on you and choose to be with my friends. It makes sense why you are so hurt and mad *when you look at it from that perspective.*"

> Karl: "It makes me think the only reason you go on dates with me when you do is because something better hasn't come up yet."
>
> Jen: "As often as I've done that, it makes sense that you would see it that way. It makes it *look like* I'm being a real jerk."

Notice that Karl is continuing on with his criticisms. One after another. Since there is still a great deal of validity, Jen listens for and acknowledges the elements of truth. She is careful to acknowledge as much truth as she can. Ultimately, Karl will run out of criticisms and naturally respond with one of the other four categories or pause. During this entire time when Jen is being criticized, Jen may or may not have a reason for why she is choosing to be with her friends instead of Karl. Responding to Karl by acknowledging the truth of the criticism might be hard for her especially if she feels she has good reason to not want to be with him. During this time she is careful to only agree with what she can *truly* agree with. Hopefully Karl will pick up on the hints of disagreement, and ask a question. Until then, Jen will wait until Karl runs out of criticisms and pauses. If there is a good reason Jen doesn't want to be with Karl and Jen would like Karl to know, she is patiently waiting for the moment when Karl asks why. She is patient because she knows that even if Karl fails to ask her why she is choosing to be with her friends instead of him, she will have an opportunity to explain soon enough. Her time to explain will come. (I'll show you this later in the chapter.) If there isn't a good reason Jen is avoiding Karl, and Jen just got caught up with selfish tendencies, all she can do at this point is to validate what Karl has experienced and take responsibility for her actions.

> "Recognizing that rude and hurtful behavior has more to do with hurts, frustrations, insecurities and weaknesses of the other, makes it a lot easier to avoid getting your feelings hurt."

Some people are afraid that if they keep agreeing with the truth of the criticisms, it's as if they are giving permission to be emotionally beat up. This is usually what a person says who doesn't really understand the process of *listening for* and acknowledging the element of *truth* and *responding only* to the element of *truth* in a criticism. Remember, "sticks and stones will break your bones..." only when they hit. And "names will never hurt you" only happens when you recognize that criticisms or name calling is actually a desperate attempt to get an emotional reaction from you. Hurtful criticisms from your spouse usually come as a result of weakness - like fatigue or lack of training or past hurts. It can also be the result of an inability to communicate insecurities, fears, hurts, disappointments and vulnerabilities appropriately. Sometimes they are the result of a natural emotion of anger. However, if there is truth to the criticism, it is important to demonstrate integrity and acknowledge it. And if it hurts when it hits, it probably should.

Getting defensive to criticisms that *aren't* true is like stepping in front of a thrown rock and saying "lucky for you I stepped in front of this rock because you could have missed me." And that would just be foolish.

If the criticizer gets stuck with one criticism after another and the amount of truth of the criticism gets smaller and smaller, this could mean they are desperate to get validated. In those cases just keep validating until they stop criticizing.

Some people are so hurt, frustrated, angry, or plagued with relational pathology that their ability to reason gets hijacked. They can't seem to understand that their pain may come from a misunderstanding of theirs. It's as if they believe that if they admit to misunderstanding or miscommunicating they will lose credibility. They desperately fight to protect their sense of credibility. For some people this is so real that they will swear on a stack of bibles that whatever happened to create the conflict wasn't their fault and couldn't be their fault. They will actually change the way they remember details. If you try to make sense of their reasoning, using their logic, it's only a matter of time until you start questioning your sanity. It's not only frustrating for you; it's really frustrating for them. They don't even know it. It's like they can't see it. They want to feel close and emotionally connected; they just don't understand why they struggle so much. Therefore, they have to believe that the reason that there is conflict is because of you.

The more afraid they are, the more they desperately cling to their devotion of being the victim. Since they don't understand that their emptiness has something to do with themselves, they stay focused on their own hurt as a way to avoid accountability and to convince the other person that they are responsible for their unhappiness and dissatisfaction. You can tell how desperate and vulnerable they are when their criticisms become irrational:

"The reason you don't love me, is because you never loved me!"

"You want me to completely lose it, so you can say it's all my fault."

"You have no idea what you are even saying. You are talking in circles and you're starting to sound crazy."

"You can't tell the difference between the truth and a lie."

"You have never been able to think for yourself."

"The reason you won't fight back is because you don't care!"

No matter how ridiculous or farfetched the criticism may be, stay true to the process of listening for and responding only to the element of truth. Avoid giving up on this process and trying to reason with them, because at this moment, they aren't reasonable. The criticizer is unwilling to really ask questions because that would put them in a vulnerable position. If they ask a question, they most likely aren't going to listen to the answer. (To know how to deal with questions, keep reading. We will get to that.) For now, just stick with validating the criticisms.

It is important to stick with the program. Do not get defensive or correct the other person. If you get defensive, the topic of conversation finally has a resting place as the energy of the conflict settles on the one issue that elicited defensiveness. Meanwhile the criticizer who is desperate for a way out of the argument finally escapes without having to take accountability.

When the critical person is stuck in the criticism, their subconscious mind says, "If I can get you to lose your cool, I've proven that you have the problem. I will feel justified in my criticisms because you are getting defensive and defensiveness is sign of guilt. If I don't get you to lose your cool, I will be compelled to ask questions to understand why you did what you did, which would give you an opportunity to point out how I misunderstood or made a mistake therefore exposing my vulnerability." This type of person experiences a variety of emotions from fear, confusion, frustration, and panic. They don't want to push their spouse away. Their ego is so fragile that they don't allow themselves to see fault in themselves. Or, they believe that if they admit they are wrong or have a fault, they are not worthy of love and therefore lose their lovability. Although they don't realize that accepting responsibility or admitting fault is actually endearing, all they feel is a tremendous amount of vulnerability. They don't realize closeness is created when they validate their spouse's frustrations. This is very scary for them. They are stuck and they need help.

This cycle can be broken. The only way to break it is to stay true to the process of dealing with criticisms as outlined in this chapter. If you abandon the process and try to correct the criticizer, you will get sucked into the argument just by trying to explain yourself. If you get defensive and say, "enough is enough" you will experience an emotional backfire because the defensiveness will be interpreted as an attempt to avoid accountability.

This is a "Catch 22" situation. Legitimately pointing out how the criticizer is mistaken will often lead to coming across as avoiding accountability, even when there is zero truth to the criticism. When the criticizer gets going on a chain of criticisms that are becoming irrational, any defensiveness, legitimate or not, will be interpreted as an avoidance strategy. The idea of someone staying loyal to being critical might sound crazy for someone who has never experienced this type of irrationality, but for those people who have experienced it, there is no doubt to its truthfulness. Hopefully, with the communication fencing techniques of this program, you can break the cycle, save yourself, save your spouse and hopefully save your marriage.

It may be helpful to know that there are two types of outcomes from the behavior of people who stay in the criticism zone. I encourage you to carefully observe how the criticizer in your life recovers from their period of irrationality. The way they come out and recover from their critical tirade will tell you a lot about them. If they recover with internal conviction, – an acknowledgment of their irrational behavior and a move for closeness with a sense of sorrow and apology, that's comforting news. This means that they are aware of their inability to stay reasonable in emotionally difficult times. It's just a matter of helping them feel safe enough to reach out and get help. And when they do, they will experience greater satisfaction, closeness, and self-confidence than they ever experienced before. If they don't recognize, or they are unreasonable and justify themselves with no remorse at all, or if they *do* know they became irrational but aren't willing to do anything about it, change is not likely to happen. If you find that you are in this situation refer to the chapter DEFINING AND ACCEPTING REALITY.

It's very easy to think that you are going crazy when you are in a relationship like this. You can take comfort in knowing you are emotionally protected when you recognize that your partner's irrational and controlling behavior is actually a symptom of desperation, insecurity or pathology. In severe forms this is emotional abuse. Having the skills to deal with this doesn't mean that you have to continue to live in an abusive relationship. If the criticism is chronic, refer to chapters 1-4 to see if there is a way to get help. If you find that you are still frustrated, and don't know what to do to change things, you will need help creating a "loving crisis" that will help you break out of a miserable stale-mate. Often times this is what needs to happen to change things for the better[3].

Parrying Declarations & Commands

The trick to parrying declarations and commands is to acknowledge the emotion or attitude.

Declarations

A declaration is a statement about how the person feels or a general statement about the situation. Declarations can come at any time in a conversation or argument. Sometimes declarations are used when there isn't any conflict. "That's a pretty sunset." "The couch looks better closer to the piano." Sometimes declarations happen when there is conflict.

"I've had it."

"I'm so mad right now."

"I try and try and get absolutely nowhere with you"

"I can't take this anymore"

"Ugh!"

Some examples of declarations as a general description of the situation would be:

"This is ridiculous!"

"This is absolutely crazy."

"That bike on the sidewalk can not be there."

[3]Email me if this situation fits you, emilharker@gmail.com.

"This is going nowhere."

"We are going around in circles."

A declaration in this context is defined as a statement about the person making the statement, or a general statement about the situation. Statements that begin with words like "we," "this" and "that" are usually good indicators that the statement is a general statement about the situation.

When the successful response to a criticism results in the criticizer making a declaration, all you have to do is identify the emotion or attitude that was exhibited by the criticizer, label it, and verbalize it. For example, if you can tell a person is frustrated when they make a declaration all you have to say is: "I can see that you are really frustrated." You don't have to be clever, witty, apologize, solve the problem, or react. All you have to do is identify the emotion or attitude used in the declaration, label it and verbalize it.

The emotion attached to declaration statements are usually going to consist of some version of anger, hurt, frustration, disappointment or betrayal. The attitude that a person expresses might be confident, sure, convinced etc. If you are unsure about what emotion or attitude they are expressing, make sure you use tentative qualifiers like *seems*, *looks like*, *appears* or *might* before the labeled emotion or attitude. For example, you might say, "I can see that you *might be* really frustrated." Or "You *seem* pretty sure that…" Please don't try to apologize at this time. It's so tempting for some co-dependent or avoidant personality types to rush to make the conflict go away by using quick apologies. If an apology is appropriate, you can do it after the person feels completely heard and understood. Your apology will be more heartfelt, heard and appreciated then. Here is a strategy to help you stay focused on listening instead of trying to make "it" go away. Try following up with a question or a prompt like, "Is that how you feel?" or "Tell me more."

Let's listen to Karl and Jen as Karl starts making declarations.

> Karl: "I've had it with feeling like you don't care!"
>
> Jen: "I can see how frustrated and hurt you might be. What is upsetting you?"
>
> Karl: "I just can't take it anymore."
>
> Jen: "You seem emotionally exhausted."

Capture the emotion in the declaration, label it, and then verbalize it. Use your own words and really try to understand. If you try to fake it and just say the words, the tone of insincerity will give you away, and your situation will go from bad to worse.

Let's see what this might sound like:

> Karl: "I've had it with feeling like you don't care!"
>
> Jen: *(with slight sarcasm)* "I'm sure you must be really frustrated."

That sarcastic statement will be an emotional zinger that really stings. It is not going to result in helping Karl feel heard and understood.

When you respond to your spouse when they make a declaration you communicate that you heard them and acknowledge what they said. You communicate that you care. This is especially useful in situations where there isn't conflict. When a person makes a declaration without asking a question, sometimes the listener will come across as if they aren't listening if they don't say something. Responding to declarations by labeling and verbalizing the emotion or attitude of the message sender will go a long way in your relationship.

Commands

The other option to a successful response to a criticism is a command. The command is simply a statement directing you to do something. Here are some examples of commands.

"Then stop it!"
"Pull your head out."
"Knock it off."
"Grow up!"
"Do something that will work."
"Change your attitude."
"Don't let it bug you."
"Quit sulking."
The threat: "If you don't Then I'll!"

Notice that these statements are literal commands of action – telling the other person to do something. Compare these statements to a criticism that sounds almost like a command. See if you can identify the words that turn a command into a criticism.

"You should stop it!"

"You need to pull your head out!"

"You need to knock it off!"

"You should try something that will work!"

Did you catch the difference? Commands that contain words like *should* or *need to* are really criticisms. Therefore, if you get one of these just treat it like a criticism and respond to the element of truth. If there is no truth, you know what to say *"What do you mean?"*

When you get a command, respond the same way you do with a declaration. Identify the emotion or attitude they used in their command, label it, and verbalize it. Commands like "ignore it," "get over it," and "let it go" have a similar emotion that is expressed. That emotion is disappointment, or frustration.

In addition to labeling and acknowledging the emotion expressed, you may want to add to your "parry" something I call "bridge building." Bridge building is connecting an emotion or attitude to an experience. Not only do you capture, label, and verbalize the emotion or attitude, you connect it to the person's experience. See if you can see how that works in these examples.

"I can see if you thought I was ignoring you last night when you were trying to talk to me, that that would seem like I don't care."

"It sounds like you are disappointed if you felt I was being unfair by not supporting you going to the movie last night?"

"It sounds like you're really frustrated with how upset I get with the people I work with and how I complain almost every day."

"I can see you are really frustrated that *I keep bringing up the same thing over and over again.*"

Do you see how after acknowledging the emotion or attitude you can decrease the likelihood of defensiveness and increase the sense of closeness? Communicating you understand that their emotion or attitude makes sense (given their perspective) can go a long way in demonstrating understanding.

Responding to commands is done the same way you respond to declarations. Let's listen to Karl and Jen in an interaction where there is a command. Karl and Jen are in the tail end of an argument where Jen is complaining that Karl's sister snubs her when they are at family parties. Jen states that she realizes she should stop complaining because it isn't getting them anywhere.

Watch how Jen responds to the command, declaration, and criticism which then leads Karl to ask a question.

Karl: "Then, knock it off!"
Jen: "You are really upset aren't you?"

Karl: "I don't know why you don't just ignore it."

Jen: "You seem disappointed that I seem to allow it to bug me."

Karl: "You're darned right! You need to grow up and let this petty stuff go!"

Jen: "I completely agree. Petty things do not deserve the energy of getting offended!"

Karl: "Well, if you know all that, why...?"

And there we have it. Finally, the criticizer asks a question where we can explain a different point of view without being argumentative. By following the next step on how to respond to questions, Jen can explain the reason why she complains. In this case Jen complains because Karl doesn't seem to notice how rude his sister is and she hopes by bringing it up to Karl he will take notice and do something about it.

A successful parry of a command will most likely end up in a criticism. No problem. You can do that all day. The good news is the longer the criticizer criticizes the faster they will run out of options. Little do they know that as they continue to go through criticisms, and declarations and commands they will either run out of things to say, or they will end up asking a question.

Parrying the Question

The trick to parrying questions is asking a question of your own: "*Do you really want to know*?"

To get to a point where you can start resolving issues you need to be able to communicate on the same level. More importantly a good solution requires mutual understanding. When the critical person asks a question it can be a sign they are ready to listen[4]. This is where we can share a different perspective or explain ourselves.

The process of responding to criticisms by carefully and completely validating the elements of truth of the criticism with a sense of confidence and calmness can create a sense of confusion in the criticizer. In this sense of confusion, the criticizer will often ask a question because they feel like they are missing something -which they probably are. Remember that a *real* question is a statement requesting information. Ideally we want the criticizer to ask a question. This is where communication actually begins. A word of caution: Prematurely volunteering an explanation before the person is done with their criticisms may not be heard—it may be attacked. In order for the criticizer to move out of attack mode and into listening mode, they need to feel understood. When the criticizer asks an honest question, it is a sign that

[4]Remember that just because a question is asked doesn't mean they are asking a question. It could be a criticism disguised as a question. That's why I wrote that "it can be a sign they are ready to listen."

they are transitioning to listening mode and are moving one step closer to mutual understanding and resolution.

Realizing that by following this communication process you will be given an opportunity to explain yourself, you can parry criticism after criticism and cope with each declaration and command with confidence and composure. Your turn to talk will come. When the criticizer finally asks a question it's understandable that you may be eagerly anticipating the question so you can give your explanation. Don't rush it. Take your time. Don't give your explanation until the criticizer has more fully transitioned from criticizer to listener. A premature explanation will be seen as an excuse. If you can tell by the pace, tone, and volume of the criticizers question that they are still very upset, you can help them transition into the listening mode by asking if they really want to know. If the criticizer really isn't ready to hear an explanation, he/she will most likely slip back into a criticism.

Betty and Brad are in the middle of an argument right now. Brad's been validating Betty's criticisms pretty well, and she asks a question. It might sound like this:

> Betty: *(Still quite upset)* So why didn't you call me when you said you were going to?
>
> Brad: Do you really want to know?
>
> Betty: It doesn't matter. I'm tired of your lame excuses. You never keep your promises anyway.

When Betty asked the question she wasn't ready for an answer. She is obviously still upset and not ready to listen. Notice how after Brad asked if she really wanted to know, she slipped back into criticism mode. When she does this, Brad listens for and responds to the element of truth. No problem.

In situations like this the person being critical will eventually ask the question again. And when they do, make sure they are really ready to listen by asking if they really want to know. You don't have to ask if they really want to know every time your spouse asks for an explanation. You only need to do this when you can tell that your spouse is really upset. If your spouse seems to be reasonable when he/she asks a question, you can go right into your answer[5].

When you respond by asking the criticizer if he/she really wants to know, the criticizer has three options. The first option is to say "no." The second option is to say "yes." And the third option is to blow through the question with another criticism, declaration, or command.

If the criticizer who asks a question say's "no," then don't waste your breath with an answer. They won't listen at that moment anyway. Saying "no" would be the equivalent of revealing they are still too upset to listen or that they are not OK with you disagreeing with them.

[5] If you answer the question and they are still upset, no problem, they will go back to one of the five statements of conflict. This time you will be prepared for them.

So, if the critical person isn't going to listen, save your answer to the time they are more able to listen. Continue listening and validating until they are ready to listen. (If they really don't care what you think, go to chapter 2.)

When you ask the person who was critical if they really want to know, you are going to hear this statement so be ready for it. "Of course I really want to know! I wouldn't be asking the question if I didn't want to know." This is very predictable if their emotions are high. It is also evidence that demonstrates they are still very upset. You can respond to this two ways. First, since what they said was a declaration you can respond by saying "You still seem pretty upset." Then, you can validate their next criticism that will usually follow. The other option you can use is to ask a follow up question. You can ask them if they are open to a different perspective or if it is OK if you see it differently. This question is especially helpful if there is a likelihood that the criticizer expects to be supported in their viewpoint or if they can't imagine there could be another perspective. Controlling, narcissistic, or even people who simply have difficulty seeing the possibility of another perspective fall into this category. This additional question "Are you open to a different perspective?" or, "Is it OK if we don't see this the same way?" communicates that there is another perspective and it compels the criticizer to make a stronger commitment to listen and hold off judgment if they really want to know.

If you ask the question, "Do you really want to

know?" and the criticizer says "yes." Make sure that the criticizer is really ready to listen. You can tell if the criticizer is ready to listen by the tone, pace and volume of their voice. You don't need to wait for the criticizer to be in a completely calm Zen state. It isn't going to happen. This isn't realistic. The reason they are loud is because they feel that they aren't being heard and that subconsciously they believe that they need to be loud to be heard. They are frustrated or angry because they are hurt, disappointed or feel misunderstood. The goal is to help them get to an emotional place where they can feel heard. Validating the truth of the criticism is one way we have already discussed to help them feel heard. Another way of helping them feel heard is to match their emotion, but just a couple of degrees lower than theirs. If your spouse is upset–their tone is edgy, their pace is quickened, and volume is heightened and you talk to them in an extremely soft and controlled voice, this could aggravate the situation. It might come across patronizing. You might think that you are providing a calming effect by your controlled tone and pace, but the other person may see you as condescending and self-righteous. If you don't take a tone that matches the seriousness of the situation you may fail to demonstrate you recognize how important this is to them. As a result they will not feel understood or trust what you say.

The third optional response to the question "Do you really want to know?" is, to blow right through your response. Often times the response is "I already know why" or "It doesn't matter" followed by a declaration, criticism or command. When this happens, just keep fencing and parrying.

Our helpful couple, Jen and Karl are about to walk out the door to go to a picnic with Karl's family. They are late again, and Karl is upset with Jen. Jen handles it like a champ. Let's listen to Karl and Jen as they walk out the door. Pay close attention to how carefully Jen parries the criticisms to the point where Karl asks a question.

> Karl: "This is just great. You are late again."
>
> Jen: "You are right. We are late again."
>
> Karl: "We are late because you took too long to get ready, again."
>
> Jen: "I can totally see how it might look like that."
>
> Karl: "Look like that? How else can it be?"

Notice how Jen expertly agrees to the element of truth without a blanket statement[6]. By agreeing with only the element of truth, she disagrees with what isn't true. This creates a sense of confusion in Karl that he feels almost compelled to ask for clarification. Jen stays true to the

[6] A blanket statement would be an avoidance tactic to end the conversation. Saying things like, "Your right" without any qualifiers is agreeing with too much of the criticism. It kills the conflict, but it also kills the closeness.

process and responds to Karl's question with a question of her own.

> Jen: "Do you really want to know?"
> Karl: "Yeah, this is going to be great!"
> Jen: "Is it OK if we disagree?"
> Karl: "Yes, fine."
> Jen: "This morning when you said we were having a picnic at the park by your sister's place, I made plans to make it there on time. But when you said that the picnic was now going to be at the park by your parent's house, it took thirty minutes out of my timeframe. You didn't tell me that the location changed until about an hour ago. But I can totally see why you would be mad because most of the time I am running late.

By carefully sorting through what was true in Karl's criticism, Jen exposed what wasn't true. In this case Jen said, "I could see how it might look like that." In other words she agreed that his opinion was understandable given his limited perspective. She wasn't defensive. She didn't try to "stand up for herself" and point out Karl's miscommunication. She patiently trusted in the process and stayed completely composed. Her response implied that there was something missing in his perception without her even having to say it. She disagreed without being disagreeable. Curiosity and confusion compelled Karl to find out what possibly could have been missing in his perspective. Even though Jen wanted desperately to get defensive and tell him how unfair he was, she stuck with the process. She carefully, sensitively, and wisely acknowledged the element of truth to the criticisms and waited for him to ask the question.

When Karl asked the question, Jen asked him if he really wanted to know to make sure that he was really ready to listen. Then she asks if it was OK for them to agree to disagree[7]. Her self-discipline and commitment to the process paid off and Jen turned what could have been an ugly explosion into a bonding moment.

But what if Karl didn't get the clue that he was supposed to ask Jen why she wasn't totally agreeing with him? Keep reading.

Silence or Pauses

The trick to parrying silence is with a question: "*Do you want to know why*?"

In working with couples and watching them interact, I have noticed that very frequently after someone

[7] I realize that there are going to be times when you don't see eye to eye on things, but those things should be rather small and a matter of taste—like what's the best ice cream flavor or whether or not tomatoes are the best food in the world. But there are some things that are based on principles and values and agreeing to disagree on these may inadvertently create distance instead of closeness.

successfully responds to a criticism, the criticizer gets so taken a-back that they get the deer-in-the-headlights look. It's as if the critical person is saying, "I'm lost, and I'm not sure where to go from here." They seem to be at a loss as to what to say or do because they have never been validated without some type of excuse or counter criticism. That befuddled moment is one description of the pause or moment of silence.

Another reason there is a pause after a criticism or declaration is because the criticizer doesn't realize there is another perspective. Sometimes the criticizer thinks that the conversation is done once they have made their point and shared their perspective. These people have the tendency to believe that if you understand, or even partially understand, then it only makes sense that you also agree. And if you agree, well... good. Conversation over. On those occasions where the criticizer doesn't get the cue to ask the question, there will be a pause, or moment of silence.

Notice that the need to be heard is so great for some people that the need for resolution is almost lost. There is no closure. No resolution. I've seen this hundreds of times. The criticizer just doesn't know what to do next. There are no changes made. No new commitments to do anything different. This isn't something that everyone does all the time, but there are some people that do it quite a lot. As you parry through the five different attacks, listen for the break in the interaction. When there is a real break in the interaction, that's the time for the communication fencing counter move. The communication fencing counter move is a question posed by the person being criticized.

"Would you like to hear how I see it?"

"Do you want to know my thoughts?"

"Would you like to know why I did what I did?"

"Would you like to hear a different perspective or different opinion?"

After asking the question, wait for a response. I've watched several couples think they are following this process but they just bulldoze ahead after asking the question. If you don't wait for a response, then you really aren't asking a question. Another point I want to make is that the question is started with the words "Would you like..." or "Do you want...`" These words have an entirely different meaning and therefore a different message compared to a similar question phrased:

"Can I tell you my side?"

"Can I tell you a different perspective?"

"Let me tell you my side."

Phrasing the question with the words "Can I ..." or "Let me tell you why ..." is asking for permission to speak. We don't want permission to speak; we want to see if the other person wants to hear. Asking the person if they want to hear, or know, requires a greater commitment to *actively* listen. This is small, but the psychodynamics are very real. I've heard that silence is golden. I would agree. Silence is the golden opportunity for you to find out if the other person really wants to understand you.

Summary

Let me simplify this process even more. There are five categories of statements in communication conflict. However there are only three responses you need to remember.

1. Criticism: If the statement is a criticism, we parry by agreeing with the element of truth. If there is zero truth we ask "What do you mean?"

2. Declaration or a Command: Capture and verbalize the emotion or attitude that was expressed.

3. Question: If it is a question, we start by asking, "Do you really want to know?"

There are some statements that may be difficult to label. For example passive aggressive statements are designed to fly under the radar. The statement "Can you see what's going on here?" is loaded with other messages. Depending on the tone, pace and context the meaning can change drastically. For the sake of an example there is an element of superiority. It has a component of condescension to it. It asks a question and simultaneously criticizes the person. It's as if the statement could be saying, "You're not getting this." "You are so dense." When you get passive aggressive statements that are loaded with allegations, criticisms, accusations, etc., simply point out your confusion. "Are you asking a question or pointing something out?" "It sounds like you are upset with me, what are you saying?"

Consider the passive aggressive statement, "Who did you have over last night?" This question is loaded with an accusation that someone come over to the house. To respond, describe the different messages you feel you are getting. "Are you accusing me of having someone over, or are you asking if I had someone over?"

Gently confronting the passive aggressive statement allows you to stay in charge instead of being sucked into becoming defensive. You are able to expose the true nature of the statement and then categorize it in one of the five statements of conflict. Once you categorize the statement, you can determine how to respond.

The following are statements in conflict. Some are combinations and some are loaded statements. See if you can identify each type of statement. Pay close attention to combinations. When you get combinations, do your best to identify one or two of the most important categories in the combo. Don't worry if you miss something. If you miss something in real life, if it is important, rest assured, it will be said again. When you apply this in the real world, treat criticisms as the trump of all the other statements. In other words, if a combination of different conflict statements contains a criticism, you would respond to the criticism as the most important component. So when there are declarations, questions and criticisms in the same breath, address the criticism first.

And before we start the practice, as they say in France, *En garde, etes-vous prêts, allez.* ("On guard. Are you ready? Go!")

"You are always making us late." (Criticism)

"You ask too much from me; you put too much pressure on me." (Criticism, criticism)

"If I make the smallest mistake, you jump all over me. You don't give me any slack." (Criticism, criticism)

"If it bothers you, ignore it." (Assumptive criticism, command)

"Don't let it bug you." (Command)

"You are so one sided; you should have married someone just like yourself. It's obvious you don't love me and think you made a mistake in marrying me because you are constantly pointing out all my flaws." (General criticism followed by a triplet of specific criticisms)

"This is going absolutely nowhere." (Declaration)

"We just keep going in circles." (Declaration)

"Do you even hear yourself talk?" (Criticism in the form of a question)

"Every time you shut down it just infuriates me." (Criticism followed by declaration)

"Would you quit lying and get your story straight?" (Criticism stated in the form of a question followed by a command)

"Just do what you always do—you are not going to listen anyway." (Command, criticism)

"Why don't you just leave? You obviously don't love me." (Question, criticism)

"I feel like what I say isn't important to you." (Declaration)

(In a sarcastic tone) – "Thanks for kissing me goodbye this morning." When you really didn't. (Passive Aggressive Criticism)

"Do you think you will ever be happy?" (Passive Aggressive Criticism)

Notice that many statements that begin with "if" are contextual statements that give you a sneak peak into the criticizer's mind. "If" statements are qualifiers that can precede commands, criticisms, questions and declarations. Instead of trying to correct the assumptions that are revealed in the "if" statement, you can use the same "if" statement qualifier in your response. For example: In the criticism "If you really aren't happy, you should leave me." Your parry to that might be, "You are right, *if* I really wasn't happy and didn't want to be with you, maybe I should." Then wait for the criticizer to say something. Don't try to correct them, or convince them, or reassure them. Also, remember to keep your tone in check. If you allow your frustration to come out in a sarcastic tone, you aren't trusting the process.

Let's see how all this works with our couple Karl and Jen. Karl and Jen have not been getting along. It's not that they have been fighting, it's just that sometimes life happens. Sometimes getting things done takes precedence over their relationship. Karl is stressed at work and Jen is stressed at home.

Let's listen to Karl and Jen as they engage in conflict. First we will listen to how the conflict might go without the application of these principles, and then we will listen to the same conflict as they both apply the principles. See if you can identify criticisms, declarations, questions, or commands. See if you can identify what makes the conflict constructive or destructive and what statements influence the difference.

Destructive Conflict

Jen: "You've been acting really offish lately. What's wrong with you?"

Karl: "You've been critical all day. Everything I do you say something."

Jen: "What? Am I supposed to just keep my mouth shut when you do things that bug me?"

Karl: "You are just being mean."

Jen: "So, it's OK for you to complain and that's being helpful, but when I say something it's being mean? That's convenient."

Karl: "You are turning this back on me?! Why am I so *not* surprised? I'm done with this."

Jen: "What's that supposed to mean?"

Karl: "It means that if you don't knock it off, I'm DONE."

Constructive Conflict

Jen: "You've been acting really offish lately. What's wrong with you?"

Karl: "You are probably right. I have been offish lately." *(Pause)* "Do you want to know why?"

Jen: "Yeah. That's why I asked."

Karl: "I guess I am just getting ready for the inevitable. If you are as miserable as you say you are, then you are going to end up leaving me."

Jen: "What do you mean?"

Karl: "Well, I hear all the time how you don't like this about me, and I do this wrong and that wrong. You're definitely not happy."

Jen: "I guess I don't realize how often I complain about things. I could see how I come across being miserable and blaming you for it, too."

Karl: "Well, if you know that, then why do you keep doing it?"

Jen: "Do you really want to know?"

Karl: "Yes."

Jen: "I know it's not right, but I guess I feel like, the only time I can get your attention is when I complain."

Karl: "Hmm. Well that would make sense. I can see now how you might see it that way."

Jen: *(silence)*

Karl: "Do you want to know my perspective?"

Jen: *(Exasperated and resigned)* "Sure."

Karl: "Seriously, do you want to know?"

Jen: "Yes. Go ahead and tell me. It sounds like you want to tell me anyway."

Karl: "I only want to tell you if you really want to know. I don't want to tell you just to tell you. I want to know if you really want to know. If you don't want to know, then why would I tell you?"

Jen: "OK, tell me."

Karl: "I see it the opposite. I feel like I can't do anything right, so I actually avoid you sometimes. You just aren't pleasant to be around. I don't mind doing things. I just don't like all the negativity. If you would be kind and nice when you talk with me I probably wouldn't avoid you so much."

Jen: "Hmm. You make a good point. I know. I can see how discouraging that would be."

Karl: "So, where do we go from here? What can we do to make our marriage better?"

This scenario isolated the principle fencing conflict separate from communicating with the desired outcome in mind. The conversation is much smoother and creates a bonding experience when you combine the principles together.

In the scenario of Jen and Karl, no resolution was made. No excuses were given. Defensiveness was replaced with understanding. Explanations were only given when the other person wanted to know. Although there were no resolutions, something more profound happened. Both felt heard and understood. This is more important than any solution.

> "Any resolution, no matter how marvelous, cannot compensate for what really creates closeness–the process."

If the process of creating a solution to the problem doesn't bring the couple closer together, they will end up growing further apart no matter how many rules they create to avoid future conflict. If the goal is greater closeness, even the most brilliant solutions, if not achieved through a process that creates closeness, will be in vain.

To further make the point. The absence of conflict is not the presence of closeness. Just like neighboring nations that share common borders may not be at war, the lack of fighting does not mean they enjoy a spirit of closeness and cooperation. Fencing conflict acts as a lighthouse of love to guide couples through the inevitable dangerous waters of conflict toward closeness and resolution.

As an untrained person, I was blown away by how random and infinite the slashes, clashes, stabs, and parries of the fencing demonstration looked. Likewise, the untrained couple in marriage conflict will be overwhelmed if they believe that the statements in conflict are infinite and random. I've demonstrated that conflict can be categorized into types of statement. If they were random, there would be no way to prepare. Fortunately for you, you are now trained to handle conflict constructively. You know now that all statements of conflict fit into a small handful of options. As a result this understanding removes the mystery of communication in times of conflict and makes what once seemed impossible possible, and what seemed impractical probable. You can now keep your cool when the relationship gets heated. By staying engaged in difficult times you can acquire mutual understanding. And with mutual understanding, you are ready to make resolutions.

The next chapter will show you how you can take any issue, and not only resolve it for good, it will make you feel closer to each other than you did before you had the argument.

Chapter 7

Disarming Landmines

> Seek first to
> understand before
> being understood.
>
> STEPHEN R. COVEY

This couple comes into my office, and I can tell from the emotional tension, they are in the final stages of an argument. Their argument seems quite rehearsed as if they have had it many times before. It was about finances and the budget. As they were wrapping up the conflict, it went something like this.

> Wife: "You have your money and I have mine. With the money you make you are in charge of the rent and the power and utilities. With the money I make, I will pay for

groceries, the cell phone, and the kids' activities."

Husband: *(upset)* "That makes it easier for me! And you can get off my case about how I spend the rest of my money."

Wife: "Fine?"

Husband: "Fine!"

Problem solved, right? If every problem this couple has results in this kind of resolution, they will probably end up as roommates.

No couple, no person for that matter will ever run out of problems. The problems are not really the problem. How couples handle problems is the problem.

See if any of these statements ring a bell? "She just keeps bringing up the same things over and over again? I'm tired of re-hashing things. Why can't we just move forward and let go of the past?" While she responds, "We never finish any conversations. The only reason it seems like I keep bringing the same thing up over and over again is because we never resolve it."

Disarming landmines resolves issues. There is no rehashing. There is no hashing at all.

The first four principles presented in this book were devoted to strategies regarding how to approach someone when you needed to say something. The next two were about how to respond to someone when there was conflict. This chapter is devoted to resolving issues once and for all in a manner that actually creates closeness.

I use the parable of "The Volleyball Court in a Minefield" to help explain the principle of DISARMING LANDMINES.

> Imagine looking out from the balcony of a beautiful home into a backyard with a nice volleyball court. The thick grass is green and inviting. There is plenty of room beyond the boundary lines. It looks like the perfect place for a volleyball court. Upon closer examination, randomly scattered on the ground are red flags with danger markings indicating where there are buried landmines. What looks like patches of sand are the scars in the field where landmines have recently been set off. What looked like a wonderful place to play volleyball looks more like a war zone.

Relationships can start looking like this volleyball court. Issues within relationships are flagged just like the volleyball court. You don't see the flags waving in the air, but they are just as real. For example there may be landmines entitled. "Don't talk about my mother." "Don't bring up finances." Heaven forbid the landmine "Don't talk about who I was before we met." The list goes on and on.

The natural process for many couples dealing with recurring conflict is to flag these landmines in an effort to avoid them. They decide that since they don't have the tools or the ability to resolve these issues, they aren't resolvable. Therefore, they do the diplomatic thing and agree to disagree!

People have varying degrees of comfort with how much closeness they can handle. Some couples can live in a relationship where there are major differences and still be comfortable. Others can't. Shared principles, values and perspectives create a sense of unity in sharing experiences together. The more differences in a couples principles, values and perspectives the more difficult the relationship can be. You will not agree on all things but in order to maximize closeness in relationships with differences, you will need to agree on most things and understand and appreciate the differences.

Discussing differences when following the process of disarming landmines can help maximize closeness even when there are times when you just can't agree. The process takes the inevitable conflict and makes it constructive and productive rather than destructive.

In some relationships no matter how hard you try, conflict arises out of substantial differences in principles. This is what Dr. John Gottman, a world renowned marriage expert, calls a "terminal flaw"- that one thing that is so important that the success of the marriage hinges on it. It is the one thing, no matter how great everything else is, that causes the whole relationship to fall apart.

It just so happens that I don't see many terminal flaws in marriages. Most problems result from how couples deal with misunderstandings. When couples worry that their values and beliefs are incongruent, they panic. They desperately attempt to reduce conflict by avoiding an argument, trying to win an argument or by trying to change their spouse's mind or come up with solutions before there is a clear understanding of each other's perspectives. A premature solution to a problem is just a setup for another problem. It's the desperate haste to solve the problem that is the problem. As soon as someone makes a point, one or both jump right into problem solving mode and start coming up with solutions.

Recently I saw a couple for premarital counseling. We will call them Chad and Amber. They had an important issue and were struggling to resolve it. The more they talked about it the more upset and frustrated they became. They both really loved each other and wanted to know if they could resolve this issue or if they were making a big mistake in getting married. They started out the normal way by taking turns complaining and using me as the mediator where both parties take turns communicating their viewpoint and then hope that in my great wisdom, I will tell them who is right and who is wrong what they are supposed to do. It demonstrates the tendency for people to rely on a solution to fix the problem. Remember the problem isn't the problem. The process is the problem.

I could tell they were starting in this direction, so I called a "time out" and suggested they follow the principles of DISARMING LANDMINES. I said instead of explaining your own viewpoint on the issue, I want you to do something completely different. I want you to explain the viewpoint or perspective of the other person regarding this issue. See if you can describe the other person's position in such a way that they can't help but be convinced that you understand what they think and feel and why.

I explained that their responsibility in the relationship was to totally understand the other person's perspective. They didn't have to agree, but they had to deeply understand the issue from their partner's point of view.

This is kind of how it went.

> Chad: *(In a slightly undermining tone)* "We were wondering if you could help us resolve a disagreement we are having about our wedding reception. Amber wants to make sure her dog is at the wedding reception, and I have a lot of problems with that. I don't think she's thinking this through all the way. Every time I tell her what my concerns are about her making a big deal about making her dog a part of the reception, she just shuts down or gets mad."
>
> Emil: "OK. It sounds like you guys are having an issue about whether or not Amber's dog should be at the reception and what role if any the dog should have at the reception. I'd like to make a suggestion that

before we try to come up with any solution or a decision about whether or not Amber's dog will be at the reception and what role her dog will play, if any, we really need to make sure we have a clear understanding of each other's perspectives about this. I am going to have you do something that isn't really normal for people to do when discussing an issue. Instead of each of you telling your own story about what your position is on the issue, I'd like you to see if you can tell your partners story in a way that they would feel comfortable with you representing their position. I want you to imagine as if you were their lawyer and really get into their heart and head on the issue. I want to see if you can see the issue from your partner's perspective better than they can. Chad, why don't you go first?"

Chad: "This is going to be hard, but let me think about this… I know that Amber's dog has been a really important part of her life over the last several years. Her dog is kind of a therapy dog for her. So she is really attached, and they have a special relationship. Almost like, well, not almost but really, like a part of her family.

At this point I cut in and had him change who he was

talking to. At first he was talking to me about Amber. I wanted him to talk to Amber.

> Chad: "She," *(turning to Amber)* "you love your dog and feel that in order for you to stay true to yourself that you want Maggie to be there and share this moment with you. Because she is part of who you are and that means she is going to be a part of this new relationship. Is that right?"

Now before Amber even tries to add to or take away from Chad's first attempt to understand Amber's position, how do you think Amber feels? Do you think she is defensive? Of course not! In fact, before I interjected Amber started "welling up" with tears. Amber feels loved and understood. She feels like her thoughts and feelings matter. This happens even if Chad doesn't agree that Maggie should be at the wedding reception. This is magic to her, and she totally softens.

> Amber: "Wow, Chad that really makes me feel good. In all our previous conversations, I never really felt that you cared about the relationship between Maggie and me. You are really hitting it on the head. I guess I want you to feel like, well, even though I know you are not that much of an animal lover, you see the love I have for Maggie and

would want her to play a role in the reception or at least want her to be there. Not just give me permission to have her there but really want her there because you love her, too. I know that may not be fair, but that's what I really want."

Chad: "So the part I was missing was the part about you wanting *me* to want it, too. Not just be OK with it, but be happy with it. Be really supportive. I mean it only makes sense that you would want me to want Maggie to be there because of how much I love you. And you really would like it if I loved Maggie and wanted her to be there too. Right?"

Amber: "Right."

So far the process was really enjoyable for both of them. Amber felt validated, understood, and loved, and Chad recognized or at least gets the feeling that although Amber loves her dog Maggie, she cares more about what he thinks[1] This makes him feel more secure and more important in the relationship.

In the real life scenario Chad did what a lot of people do. As soon as he felt like he understood Amber's perspective he started exploring solutions. As soon as he started going in this direction, I stopped them because

[1] If Amber really did care more about her dog Maggie, I would refer Chad back to chapter 2 DEFINING AND ACCEPTING REALITY.

I knew that although Chad might be able to resolve the issue, the closeness they want to have isn't about resolving the issue it's about, understanding, and intimacy. It's about going through the process for both of them. If Chad came up with a solution they would miss out on the closeness that comes from Chad feeling understood by Amber. So far, Chad has been able to communicate to Amber in a way that makes her feel understood. But Amber hasn't really done the same for Chad. This part is especially important because this is where a lot of men and the fixers of the relationship get sidetracked from the relationship and move right on to the solution.

I asked if Amber felt understood, and when she said she did, I asked Amber to see if she could describe Chad's thoughts and feelings about having Maggie at the reception. Turning to Chad Amber said:

> Amber: "Well, let me see if I can do this. I guess the big thing is that I have been making a big deal about wanting Maggie at the reception probably to the point that it could come across that I want her there more than I want you there and that wouldn't feel very nice. Also, we haven't decided on a place to have the reception, and we may choose a place that may not be that accommodating for Maggie. So the more I push to have Maggie there at the reception, the more I can see that I'm kind of pushing this on to you. Is

that it?"

Chad: "Yeah, that's pretty much it. I'm really glad that you have Maggie, but I don't want our wedding reception to turn into a reception for Maggie and distract from the importance of celebrating our wedding. So the more you were talking about how important it was to have Maggie at the reception, the more I felt like Maggie was more important than me. However, I totally understand that isn't the case. And talking to you now has made that clear. I think something else that worries me is that we are going to have a lot of different people there at the reception, and there may be some people who aren't comfortable with Maggie running around. So I want to make sure that people are comfortable and have a great time at the wedding reception."

Amber: "Oh yeah! I can totally see how that could be a big concern. If Maggie is wandering around, there could be small kids that are afraid of dogs even though Maggie would not hurt them at all. But there could also be people who are allergic to dogs, too. And that wouldn't be comfortable either. I wasn't really thinking about that. Is there still something I am missing?"

Chad: "No, you pretty much got it."

At this point both were holding hands. I asked them how they were feeling about the process they were going through. Both reported that they were really feeling closer and more cared about than before they had the conversation. I pointed out that by going all the way through this process of dealing with conflict both were able to share their thoughts and feelings, and experience greater closeness instead of distance. What's most interesting is that they felt closer to each other than they did before they started talking about the issue and the problem wasn't even resolved!

Even though Chad could have resolved this on his own without having the chance to share his perspective, having Amber really understand more about what he was thinking and feeling made a big difference in Amber's perspective. But more importantly, it provided a way for both of them to experience a greater sense of understanding and feeling of closeness.

It is complete foolishness to fix a problem without understanding the problem. Men, how many times have you tried putting something together or fix something that wasn't working only to find out that the real problem wasn't what you thought it was? As a result, you spent more time and money on the thing than if you would have just taken a few more minutes to read the instructions or really figure out what was wrong. Women, how often have you made suggestions to your children, or a friend to help them with a problem without really understanding what they really needed? As humans, we really want to make life better. We think the best way to stop the pain is by making the problem go away. I hope you realize now that problems aren't the problems. The real problem is the myopic focus on creating a solution. The real solution is to focus on the process. The resolutions will come when you understand the issues.

A *landmine* is an issue that you keep talking about, but aren't able to resolve. The "relational landmine" has a lot of negative energy around it and reduces the level of satisfaction and fulfillment in life. It also reduces the amount of life energy available for creativity and coping with everyday stress. If the landmine isn't disarmed, it sucks energy away from other things in life, which increases the likelihood of getting irritated and frustrated with your spouse. And when people are irritated and frustrated, they say things that could create a chain reaction of pain and misery. The uneducated way to handle these situations is to engage in an emotional debate, which will result in more hurt feelings and sleeping on the couch.

Unlike real landmines, relationship landmines have a way of resetting themselves after they have blown up. The only way to move freely without fear is to disarm the landmines for good.

Disarming landmines uses the skills and abilities acquired through the application of the principles of the other techniques. It requires people to truly put the interests of the other above their own and see situations through the eyes of their partner. The process builds trust.

There are five steps to DISARMING LANDMINES. The first step is *Defining the Landmine* . The landmine is the issue you want to resolve. Defining the landmine is best done by filling in the blanks of this statement. "When this (__________) then this (__________)." This is how you identify what you think the problem is. For example: "When you *leave your clothes on the floor*, [then] it *makes me feel like you expect me to pick them up*." Often times the problem is too vague. When this happens, and it will, don't worry. Just refine the problem as you go through the process. When you refine it, just start over with the process. I encourage you to avoid taking shortcuts. Taking shortcuts in this process will actually make the process take longer. Remember the focus in not on solving the problem but on the process. Just focus on the process.

After defining the land mine, the next step is to define the perspective of the "other" person regarding the issue. Instead of explaining your own viewpoint on the issue, explain the viewpoint of your spouse.

After you make an honest attempt to understand your spouse's perspective, check in to see if you are missing anything. This is where your spouse fills in what you've missed or emphasizes important points. After your spouse fills you in, reiterate what he or she added using your own words. Then you ask again. "What else am I missing? Do you feel understood?" This process continues until your spouse tells you they feel understood. Remember, the point is to understand, not agree[2]. Be your spouse's voice on the issue and then give your spouse their voice on the issue. It is important to do your best to understand your spouse's perspective before you ask if you missed anything. This step requires a more emotional and psychological investment and helps override your natural defensiveness. Understanding through interrogation is not loving and supportive. If you are the second person in this situation and don't feel like the other person agrees with you, that is OK. The point is to feel like the other person understands.

The next step is for the spouse that feels understood to understand their spouse - just reverse roles. As soon as you feel your spouse understands your perspective that's your cue to see if you can explain how your spouse sees the problem. You follow the same steps as described earlier. After you have made an honest attempt to understand the perspective of your spouse, you "check in" by asking if there is something that you are missing. Your spouse then validates what you got right and makes any corrections or additions to your description. This continues until your spouse is convinced that you understand their perspective. When both people feel understood and all the important information is on the table,

[2]Like we mentioned in the previous chapter, some people have a hard time feeling understood if you don't agree with them. If you get that feeling, simply ask if they feel like you need to agree with them in order for them to feel like you understand.

you can move on to resolving the issue.

This next step is one of the biggest components to what makes this communication and conflict resolution program different than any other communication program I've ever seen or heard about. When a person makes a resolve, they are making a promise—a promise to themselves. So if you are going to resolve an issue, you are going to make a promise to do something to make the problem not be a problem anymore. It is not based on a compromise or a quid pro quo agreement. "If you do this, then I'll do that." The resolve in this program is a promise of "I will do *this* no matter what you do." The normal quid pro quo agreement is doomed at the very start. It usually ends up with: "Why didn't you do this?" or "Well, I didn't do this because you didn't do that." And that is not going to resolve anything.

So when it comes to resolving the issue, the first person (who started the conversation) figures out their resolve to prevent the conflict from ever happening again. This resolve is independent of the other person's resolve. It does not rely on anything the other person does, and this is for good reason. I've already pointed out one of the problems with the compromise or the quid pro quo resolution. I'll explain the other reason in just a minute. After the first person writes out their resolve, the second person shares their resolve.

I want to emphasize the importance of a personal and independent resolution. Resolving issues is a promise individuals make to single-handedly kill the problem. This is vitally important. When both people promise to do something to resolve the problem independently of what the other person will do, the backup plan is built in. It prevents an argument even if the problem comes up again. With independent resolutions from both parties, the only way for this issue to be an issue again is for both people to simultaneously fail to keep their promise. This approach significantly reduces the chances of failure because the couple is double covered. And if both people default on their resolve, they can independently take full responsibility for their failure. Imagine an argument where both people are trying to convince the other person that the reason that the problem came up again was because of their own personal failure to follow through with their promise. An argument where both people are trying to convince the other person that they blame themselves for the problem is an argument that I can live with.

To make the process crystal clear, here is an example of Kevin and Susie disarming a landmine. Kevin and Susie have been married for 16 years. Every time Kevin comes home from work he yells out in a friendly, energetic tone: "I'm home! Where is everyone?" Susie hates it when he does this. She usually says something under her breath and gives him the cold shoulder. After learning this program Kevin decides to see if he can make this problem go away.

Kevin: "I've noticed that we have a land-

> mine here. When I come home and shout, 'I'm home where is everyone?' you keep getting mad at me."

Notice, this is simply stated. There is no sophistication here. It's simple. Since Kevin is labeling the landmine, he is the first one to try to understand the perspective of his wife, Susie.

> Kevin: "I'd like to see if I understand why you get so upset when I do this. I think you are annoyed because it seems that I am inconsiderate of others. For example, you might be in the middle of something when I come in from work. Maybe you are having a conversation with someone or someone is trying to get some rest. Is that why it bothers you?"

He is still focusing on the wife's perspective in his last statement when he "checks in."

> Susie: "Yes! When you come home, you don't stop to think if there is a visitor or if the baby is sleeping. It is as if no-one else in the house matters except you, and when you continue to do it, even after I tell you how upset I get, I feel totally unimportant! Plus, I really enjoy the peace and quiet of being home."

Now Kevin reiterates what Susie said in order to demonstrate that he truly understands her perspective. This part is very important and often overlooked. The husband shouldn't just say, "I understand," or "OK got it." If he gets it, he needs to tell her in *his own words* showing her that he has integrated her message into his soul. Just saying the words is just parroting.

> Kevin: "So part of the reason you are upset is that I don't stop to think about what everyone else is doing. I'm just thinking about myself. So underscore inconsiderate. And when I barge in all loud and obnoxious, I ruin the peace you were in. Is that right?"
>
> Susie: "Right."

So far, this whole step is devoted to understanding Susie's perspective. It validates and supports her point of view. After feeling understood, Susie can transition into trying to understand Kevin's viewpoint. Instead of just asking him what his perspective is, she becomes Kevin's voice first and then checks in to give Kevin his voice to modify what she said[3].

[3]Susie picking up after feeling understood is the ideal process. This doesn't happen all the time. If Susie doesn't try to understand Kevin's perspective, Kevin can ask Susie if she wants to know. If she says yes, Kevin can say, "I tried to understand your perspective, would you mind giving it a shot? I'd like to know how you would describe what my perspective is." If Susie says "no" refer to chapter 2 DEFINING AND ACCEPTING REALITY.

So, she starts out by saying:

> Susie: "OK, let me see if can understand this situation from your perspective. You come home after a hard days' work. You want to be a part of what is going on in the house. You like knowing what everyone is doing and where everyone is. You are just trying to check in, and then I give you a hard time when you do it. Is that right?"
>
> Kevin: "Yes, it is just…I hate being away from the family as much as I am and I am excited to be home and spend time with the kids and be a part of their lives. I feel an urgency to connect, maybe that's why I keep doing it even though I know it bothers you."

Susie reiterates what Kevin says.

> Susie: "So you're really not trying to be obnoxious. You are just excited to be home and you want to connect with the kids. Is that right?"
>
> Kevin: "Right."

At this point, both Kevin and Susie feel understood. Their emotional guards and defenses are down. With all the information on the table they are able to create a resolution. At this point they consider what they could do to independently make sure that this issue is resolved for good. They approach the solution as if they will single-handedly resolve the problem and make it a non-issue in the future[4]. In this case, Kevin says:

> Kevin: "To prevent this from ever happening again, I am going to check in with you to find out what is going on and where everyone is before I get home. Once I'm home, I can go around the house checking in with everyone. I can do this with a phone call before I come home or I can do it from the driveway before I come in the front door. If we can't connect on the phone, I will quietly go through the house and connect with the kids."

Notice, if Kevin did this, he would single-handedly prevent this problem from every happening again. But we don't stop there like so many conversations end, we go on to Susie's resolution.

> Susie: "When the garage door opens, that gives me just enough time to take a

[4]Some issues are really hard for people to figure out what they can do independently to make the problem go away. If I included all the possibilities, the book would be too long. Go to EmilHarker.com and click on the Book Forum section to bring up your personal issue, or email me at emilharker@gmail.com.

> minute to greet you and check in with you to let you know what is going on and where everyone is. I can also call you at 5:30 PM when I know you are on your way home."

Again, if the husband didn't do his part, but she did her part, the problem would be solved.

For many people these types of conversations are really hard to have because of the emotional baggage that leads to emotional squirrel chasing. In other words, talking about one issue brings up another issue and then another, until you can't remember what you were talking about in the first place.

In order to make this process easier, I encourage you to start by writing this process out. Keep a journal or notebook and call it your DISARMING LANDMINES notebook. As you become more comfortable with the process, you can apply the steps in a face-to-face dialog. I've made a workbook to help you develop these skills. Included in the workbook are worksheets guiding you through the DISARMING LANDMINES process. You can go to Emilharker.com for a digital download or to order a printed one.

The more you practice the better you will get at identifying problems and resolving them. You will be able to communicate smoothly and naturally even in times of conflict. Instead of walking on egg shells when there is an issue, you have a process that makes you feel like you are walking on clouds. As you work together applying these principles, as you share your thoughts and ideas, YOU CAN TURN CONFLICT INTO CLOSENESS.

Chapter 8

Final Thoughts

Having a healthy marriage is much like having a healthy body. If you don't exercise your muscles, they will atrophy and be nothing but dead weight. Your muscles will not be able to support you or give you the strength to live and move. The same thing occurs within a marriage. When you work on your marriage, it can't help but get stronger. A magical marriage only seems like magic because of the constant dedication to making your marriage a priority. The positive energy creates momentum of more positive energy.

By applying these relationship and communication strategies for creating a great marriage, it won't matter what kind of issues or problems you face as a couple. You will face each problem together. Each potential conflict is an issue that has the potential to bring you closer together. I challenge you to take your relationship and yourself to the next level by committing to learning *The 7 Communication Skills of Successful Marriages* and join the growing club of great marriages. If you have enjoyed this book, support me in my mission and share this book with your family and friends. We will need to work together to make a difference in our community.

It is my mission to provide you the most powerful programs and tools to make your relationship amazing. If you need help learning how to use the tools, please contact me. For more helpful tools and a forum to share your stories and get inspired for marital greatness please visit emilharker.com. If you have any questions or comments about this program please email me directly at emilharker@gmail.com.

About the Author

I'm a husband, father, brother and son. I love to cook and I love food. (That's actually my first real love.) I have three boys and we love spending our summers on Lake Powell and camping in the Utah mountains. I've been married for almost 20 years now to a woman I love dearly.

It hasn't been easy. You can ask my wife and she will tell you that there are many times when she wishes I was a massage therapist instead of a marriage therapist! I decided to become a relationship therapist because I love people. I was the guy in high school the girls would talk to about their terrible boyfriends. I was fascinated about relationships. I wondered why people did what they did, what caused people to be depressed, anxious. I wondered what made relationships work? So, when I took a psychology class in college, I was bit by the bug. I dove right in and immersed myself into studying.

I love what I do. I feel honored and privileged to be invited into the most sacred part of peoples lives. I enjoy teaming up with my clients to help them discover their true selves and empower them to reach their potential.

When I'm not presenting, or writing, or building programs, or seeing clients, I'm probably with my kids or my brothers and their kids cooking in the kitchen, playing outside, or cuddling on the couch watching movies.